"A Heart of Ideality in My Realism"
and Other Essays on Howells and Twain

LOCUST HILL LITERARY STUDIES
No. 9

"A Heart of Ideality in My Realism" and Other Essays on Howells and Twain

John E. Bassett

LOCUST HILL PRESS
West Cornwall, CT
1991

Library of Congress Cataloging-in-Publication Data

Bassett, John Earl, 1942-
    "A heart of ideality in my realism" and other
essays on Howells and Twain / John E. Bassett.
       166p.   cm. -- (Locust Hill literary studies: no. 9)
       Includes index.
       ISBN 0-933951-36-1 : $30.00
       1. American fiction--19th century--History and criticism.
2. Howells, William Dean, 1837-1920--Criticism and interpretation.
3. Twain, Mark, 1835-1910--Criticism and interpretation.
4. Realism in literature. I. Title. II. Series.
PS374.R37B37 1991
813'.40912--dc20   90-46908
                                       CIP

Printed on acid-free, 250-year-life paper
Manufactured in the United States of America

In memory of
my mother
Frances Walker Carnduff

Contents

Foreword

Most of these essays grow out of a study, over the last seven years, of the concern of writers in nineteenth-century America with their own authority and with the cultural and epistemological authority of different forms of literature. I have focused on Howells and Twain because they were the first strong writers in America to set out to be a success along the lines of the new entrepreneurial model and to succeed in doing so. Some of the same issues have already been explored in relation to earlier periods of American literature, by Emory Elliott, Eric Sundquist, and others.

After an introduction putting Howells and Twain in a wider context, four essays consider writings of Howells. One analyzes his early reviews, those written before he attained the status of major novelist and revealing some of his aesthetic and social uncertainties and ambivalences. The Howells of this period was still groping towards his later notion of Realism and was not yet the confident self-mythographer of *Literary Friends and Acquaintances*. My next three essays deal with Howells' first three novels, in which like Henry James he developed a new kind of fiction growing out of the romance tradition. These essays comprise part of a fuller book solely on Howells, and perhaps some day it will be written, exploring the basis for signification and fictional meaning throughout a long and influential career.

Twain meanwhile was mining a totally different vein and was flaunting the position of the writer, not developing an aesthetic of representationalism in which the author would be effaced from his text. The last nine essays in this book deal with Twain, seven revolving around a concern with literary authority and, in Twain's case, the power latent in performance. Two essays on *Huckleberry Finn* fall into a different category. One, "*Huckleberry Finn*: The End Lies in the Beginning," may in a subtle way have generated all the other essays in my book. It is one of several justifications of the ending of *Huckleberry Finn*, suggesting that Twain's conclusion was latent in the first part of the book; here it is followed by an essay that may seem to contradict it, at least by temporarily minimizing the importance of justifying the ending. Perhaps the two together represent the best overall approach to the novel, a drive to explicate the structure satisfactorily along with a recognition that the novel was composed at separate times of Twain's career. The third essay on *Huckleberry Finn* addresses a recurring pedagogical problem of teaching it to racially mixed classes, but raises along the way a number of related questions about canons, meaning, and authority.

I wish to thank Charlene Turner and Virginia Aldridge for their help in typing the manuscript. The assistance of Robert Hirst at the Bancroft Library, University of California, was most helpful to my work on Twain, as was the assistance of David Nordloh at Indiana University to my work on Howells. The library staffs on two campuses—and in particular George Masterton at Wayne State University and Ann Baker Ward at North Carolina State University—have always been the kind of professionals on which all good research in the humanities depends. My initial interest in some of the issues in these essays goes back to ideas suggested many years ago by Benjamin Spencer and Howard Horsford, and as usual I am grateful for their instruction. Allen Stein has always shown an interest in discussing Howells and Twain with me and has patiently encouraged me to reconsider several unsubstantiated arguments. Finally, my family has helped in numerous small and large ways.

Acknowledgments

I wish to acknowledge those journals in which these essays previously appeared: *Papers in Language and Literature* for "'A Heart of Ideality in My Realism': Howells' Early Criticism" (1989); *Studies in the Novel* for "*Their Wedding Journey*: In Search of a New Fiction" (1987) and "*The Gilded Age*: Performance, Power, and Authority" (1985); *Nineteenth-Century Literature* for "*A Chance Acquaintance*: How Fiction Would Mean" (1985) and "*Roughing It*: Authority Through Comic Performance" (1988), © The Regents of the University of California; *Mississippi Quarterly* for "Tom, Huck, and the Young Pilot: Twain's Quest for Authority" (1985); *American Literary Realism 1870–1914* for "*Huckleberry Finn*: The End Lies in the Beginning" (1984); *Free Speech Yearbook* (Speech Communication Association) for "Huck and Tom in School: Conflicting Freedoms and Values" (1989); and *Western American Literature* for "*Life on the Mississippi*: Being Shifty in a New Country" (1986). The other essays appear here for the first time.

"A Heart of Ideality in My Realism"
and Other Essays on Howells and Twain

1

By Way of Introduction:
Twain, Howells, and the
Authority of Writers in America

The strongest post-Civil War American writers were in curious ways unperceptive of economic and social realities. William Dean Howells, Mark Twain, Henry Adams, and Henry James, despite remarkable achievements, retained a set of blinders that narrowed their vision and blocked out significant aspects of issues they raised. Their world was changing rapidly, and the changes dislocated writers who had grown up in a pre-war America where village and rural norms still seemed dominant. The worlds of Hawthorne and Melville—to say nothing of Balzac, Eliot, and Verga—were also transitional; and although they could not reconcile the contradictions of their age, they often defined issues with more perception. James to some extent did also, but in exchange for personal exile, separation from social changes that Howells and Twain at least partially confronted, and a pragmatic narrowing of subject matter. While James was fleeing America's new literary marketplace, Adams was beating back into the past to times when his own family had authority, times over which he as expert chronicler could exert a new authority through writing. Twain adopted a performer's mask and used it in imaginative ways to control audiences and subject matter. Howells operated behind the most deceptive aesthetic convention of all—Realism.

In part American writers were unable to step outside several frameworks of perception—an individualistic ethos, with diverse strands back through Emerson and common-sense philosophy and Franklin and the Reformation, and with its new accommodation to business progressivism; a nostalgic agrarian model of virtue, supplemented by frontier publicity; and a notion of America's manifest specialness. Even when a novel had a businessman as hero, such as Christopher Newman or Silas Lapham, he had non-urban origins and views, and there was little sense of factories, laborers, or anything urban or industrial that might symbolize a positive value. In some ways it was in the writers' own self-interest to see and present America as they did; moreover, Twain and Howells were the first two Americans to set out from the start to succeed in letters as serious writers, according to the model of entrepreneurial individualism in the ascendant, and to achieve that success. Achieving that success required certain other accommodations; and these can best be understood within a general pattern of nineteenth-century American writers having a sense that they were not significant participants in social change and developing strategies to overcome that handicap.

The problem most frequently discussed by American writers before the war was the lack of an international copyright that included American writers. Journals of the day are full of petitions and arguments on the issue. In part the matter was simple economics. Easily pirated European texts reduced demand for copyrighted native books; pirated American texts abroad further cost writers their deserved royalties. An international copyright, of course, was a complex tariff, generating no federal revenues but raising consumer prices to reward native writers. Unlike the Tariff of Abominations, it did not pass Congress. The reluctance of a republican legislature to approve it implicitly affirmed the dispensibility of literature as a native industry in America. A nation valuing engineers and the "useful arts" paid more attention to the incentives in its patent policies than in its copyright policies.

The problem is at times explained as a simple consequence of capitalism, which turns workers and consumers into a set of functions and commodities; but while that may be partly true, the pattern was different in America. European countries had a tradition of classes for which imaginative literature and the play it fostered were assimilated conventions of life. The newer middle classes discovered in the novel a form that could validate a new myth of its own justification and in literary discourse a mode of assimilation into the established classes. In America, however, there was no such tradition, certainly not for native writers. Except for pastors to their own congregations, and political writers at the time of the Revolution, writers would have at best an undefined notion of whom they wrote for, unless—like Beverley, Byrd, or Irving—they wrote for an English audience. American readers—and if a nation of shopkeepers Americans were also a nation of readers—were satisfied with English and classical texts; and as any sense of a significant past or cultural identity was more English than American, it is not hard to see why most Americans felt little need for an American book. Even as they were convinced to value an "American Literature" as a patriotic entity, they might feel little need to read an American book. Moreover, several English writers were good and when critical of social institutions they were safe in America because their objects of criticism usually were "over there."

When Dickens, or Cooper, directed his barbs at restless Americans, there was no confident mode of reaction and response. The demand for a national literature, however, was part of a strategy by which writers—and editors—in America tried to establish a position of authority from which they might influence events and thereby achieve some power.

Washington Irving wrote for an English audience more than an American. He was a popular and honored writer in America, but his implied audience was like that of Goldsmith. William Cullen Bryant more or less stopped writing poetry, though he became regarded as the best American poet, after assuming an influential position in journalism; and in a sense newspapers provided a writer in 1830 with a clearer sense of authority and purpose than did poetry or fiction. Emerson secularized the sermon, and sought his audience in his sense of the congregation. At a time when the oratory of Webster, Calhoun, and Clay seemed more influential and significant than anything pastors said from the pulpit, Emerson's departure from the pulpit was as dependent on his sense of the loss of authority of the church as on the nature of the Eucharist. His protest against joint stock companies was a measure of his awareness of business's increasing control over American life; but in an age concerned with constitutions, declarations, and laws derived from oratorical skill, it was not surprising that he could believe in the authority of the word. A good Whig in his politics, he still valued a self-reliant individualism as a gospel to justify the speaker-writer: the authority of persuasion would replace that of tradition and that of fiscal power.

Hawthorne was the one who set out to be a writer. *Fanshawe* and early plans for collections of tales reveal him groping for a form and audience with Irving and some English novelists in mind. The vogue of faculty psychology, the Lockean-Kantian debate, romantic idealism all provide intellectual contexts for understanding Hawthorne; but the literary record is one of great uncertainty about readers and publishers. The much discussed ambiguity and ambivalence of his stories is partly due to the uncertain communicative function they were performing. Hawthorne was a moral commentator without a clear sense of congregation, a fictionist with an unclear readership, Bunyan without a church. He would gladly have been a success like Twain and Howells, but to be it would never have been a platform performer like Twain; and in his day literary editorships paid almost nothing and did not provide the influence that the *Atlantic* or *Harper's* or *Scribner's* later did.

Some men turned to editing, and either like Nathaniel Willis and George Morris eked out a living, or like Poe and Simms failed to eke one out. Then there was Melville, who stopped writing when he realized he had no audience or that what audience he had was not reading his novels as he had written them. If *Pierre* has a dimension of authorial self-pity amid its turgidly self-reflexive message, *The Confidence Man* is in part an

aggressive assault on its readers. "Dollars damn me," he once wrote
Hawthorne, but had no Twain to teach him how to adjust to that fact of
life. Failure, with a Byronic pose, was the only course for a writer moti-
vated by Calvinistic moralism and a romantic aesthetic. A more dialecti-
cal thinker than most writers in America, he had in 1857 no way out of
the writer's dilemma. The turn away from prose to poetry seems to have
been a final search for a marriage of form, message, and audience.

Whitman, an exact contemporary, found his medium as Melville lost
his. He confirmed the Americanist message of Emerson with an empirical
basis. He enshrined the sensual particulars of America, some of which
threatened his more genteel contemporaries, who might also be boosting
America as an advance on the corruptions of Europe. He seems to have
misperceived his potential audience; but likely his dream of a poetry *for*
the common man as well as *of* the common man was more useful as romantic model than as actual condition. He did seek an audience different
from that of either Lydia Sigourney and the sentimental versifiers of the
day or Longfellow and the Cambridge poets, for like Twain later he knew
that popular writing of the day had no authority, and in the eyes of many
Americans was a female refuge and ornament in a male business world
denying any serious communicative function for poetry or fiction. Whitman did not validate the middle-class business world but rather a new
democratic myth of individual artisans, farmers, craftsmen, and sailors all
performing their trades and making up America. Missing from the myth is
that spreading commercial network rendering independent workers secondary to its own needs. More than any other American writer, except
perhaps Howells, Whitman depended on and asserted the specialness of
the American experience. The myth informed the poem, but from then on
the poem would inform the continuing myth; and like Emerson's "Self-
Reliance," Thoreau's *Walden*, and Twain's *Huckleberry Finn* it could be
utilized to reinforce the structures their authors thought they were ques-
tioning.

Leaves of Grass defines an authority for American poetry for the only
time in our history, at least for a poetry that does not admit either its
separateness from the workaday world or its impotence. As Melville was
admitting the impossibility of writing, Whitman was reauthorizing it for a
few years on a Jacksonian basis, but accepting also the need for the writer
to be the promoter, the image—one of the roughs—inscribed in his own
text as a pluralistic, kaleidoscopic I. The Civil War exploded the romance—even "Passage to India" is no longer a paean to America—not
only because it disunified the myth but also because it clarified the conquest of America by industrial capitalism.

That is where Howells and Twain came in, or rather ran out—to
Venice and Nevada—when the shooting began; but before turning to
them, a few more examples may help to clarify the problematic situation

of the American writer after 1865. Longfellow had accepted the diminished function of the poet, to while away the little interludes of life after a rough business day, with the reward of international popularity. He had not set out to be a poet. Ambitious, he became a successful academic and success in poetry came later. Whittier drew on a firm notion of the moral and religious functions of verse, unaware that it lacked credibility and influence in his day. Like Bryant he secured most of his public identity as a journalist. Meanwhile the popular novels of Susan Warner, Maria Cummins, and Emma Southworth were gathering a new audience for fiction. At the same time Harriet Beecher Stowe used the sentimental romance to justify liberal Christianity against a sterner Calvinism and to validate a middle-class domestic myth threatened by slavery and atheism. She was taken seriously, moreover, if not exactly in the ways she intended. She did not anticipate being banned in the South, and in fact felt she and Southern women could reason together. Her general portrayal of Southerners is sympathetic. If she misjudged one audience, however, she aimed well otherwise: a popular outlet, the *National Intelligencer*, and then careful marketing of the book version of *Uncle Tom's Cabin*. She was, like her future neighbor Clemens, keenly attentive to literary marketing.

After the end of slavery, however, Stowe, like other Northerners, had a hard time adjusting her social and literary vision. The cause was won, slavery destroyed. Not liberal Christianity but industrial capitalism, however, was in the saddle and controlled the Republican Party, a necessary club for all "good" people. In the face of the Democratic Party's disgrace, it defined itself as the heir of the Washington-Jefferson patriotic tradition. If a good Democrat like Whitman could articulate his estrangement from post-war trends, in *Democratic Vistas*, a good Republican like Stowe might have to retreat, unable to center her writing in the new ethos or to write against it. A sense of audience in one way similar to that felt by Stowe seems to have operated for John William DeForest. He used fiction to articulate a liberal enlightened vision of America against extremes of puritanism and romanticism, and against political corruption. In novels such as *Witching Times, Miss Ravenel's Conversion from Secession to Loyalty, Kate Beaumont*, and *Honest John Vane*, he set a sensible but at times dull reasonableness against a more attractive or popular demagoguery or cavalier romanticism, and oscillated between hope and despair as to which would prevail. He never achieved a large audience, perhaps as some say because he wrote for a more masculine audience than America then offered, or perhaps because he was not a good promoter. A decade or so after the war he stopped writing, apparently feeling—as Melville had—that he had lost his audience. By then the writer in America was going off in new directions.

The category "writer" itself is troublesome. Religious, scientific, and social commentary was normally alternated in journals with poetry and literary criticism, and was itself "literature" for its readers. Modern critics have narrowed the term to emphasize poetry, fiction, and certain rhetorical prose and to define a specific continuity, but writers themselves did not quite think of their work within that same framework. Academic criticism and scholarship has further blurred the function of writing in America after the Civil War. Realism has often been evaluated as a reflection of American life of the period, and writers as setting out to capture life as it was and to embody significant moral questions within representative stories of reasonably typical figures. Although most criticism of fiction at that time emphasized its moral effect on readers, academics have played down such a participatory function of these books in the interests of matters related to artistic unity, influences, and traditions. If a scholar is not commended for illustrating a previously unappreciated unity, she is generally for connecting a novel to an accepted ethical position of today and thereby raising its status for that reason. The consequence may be, however, to separate us further from the writers of the period, their problems and intentions.

It is hard today to visualize Twain and Howells at the beginnings of their careers, for in each case dozens of books intervene and volumes of literary history rewrite those books. The institutions of writing and publishing are much changed. Neither man set out to write the way a young person would today with clear generic traditions, critical vocabularies, and publishing outlets. Both later in life penned autobiographies that made it seem they had been destined only for the one career; and maybe given their childhoods around printshops and books, their youth around newspapers, and their intense ambition, it is true. But Howells, author of forty novels, had no sense he would be a novelist until he was over thirty, and as a youth was unsure how anyone might make a living as a literary man at all. For some time after the war he was described as a budding poet not a writer of fiction. Twain never did want to be a novelist. In his late twenties he was developing his own brand of humorous journalism, but seems only haltingly to have considered how to combine his skills with "serious" writing to make a career satisfying his ambition.

Both were young men on the make with their eye on wealth and status, even as they were also serious about reading and writing. They were perhaps more conscious of their writing as communication than as art, both being trained as journalists with one eye always on their audience. Their success as literary promoters after the war was in part due to this sensitivity to audience. They had to secure a democratic patronage in a market economy. Lacking the older forms of patronage of an aristocracy or gentry, they had to create or discover an audience themselves.

Howells at first seems to be a bit like Hawthorne in that at an early age he committed himself to a life in letters of some sort. A bookish son of a Swedenborgian father, he appears to have lacked only a sense of how one would make a living from such a first love. Such at any rate is the image we get from the retrospective autobiography of a grand old man of fiction, not our necessary inference from documents of the 1850s. As a journalist and hopeful poet, Howells admired the German poet Heine for his dreamy melancholy mood, but was relatively unappreciative of his satire and his political radicalism. Howells' published poems were pallid and unoriginal. His first published prose book was a campaign biography of Abraham Lincoln, not important to the election of 1860 but sufficient to qualify as patronage-writing and to give Howells some sense of involvement in the progress of his country. When he returned from Venice after the war he published two travel books and over time worked himself into a position as Editor at *Atlantic Monthly*. In that position he wrote numerous reviews of poetry, fiction, and other prose. Gradually he developed a notion of an American fiction that might validate a new middle-class American type of life and within it a significant position for the writer-observer. It was a fiction privileging values he associated with a genteel tradition, within which in retrospect he embedded his own career, but it was located in a world that industrial capitalism had altered. On the one hand, Howells valued fiction about life the author observed, and over which like the social scientists he could be a professional master; on the other hand, much that an author might observe should be omitted. Howells desired an America in which the dehumanizing force of capital would be moderated so that a fresh r(R)epublican national spirit could restore the world lost in the war. That world, unlike the actual commercial world around Howells, would value and not merely commodify the discourse of a writer, which itself would not have to be the debased coinage of Josiah Holland or Elizabeth Stuart Phelps in order to have currency. What Howells at first failed to see was that even in his own position of authority—arbiter of a significant cultural periodical—he was a commodity: a "safe" steward for the Lowell-Holmes class, itself declining yet never fully accepting the Howellses as equals; a relatively safe editor to preserve respectability in a journal read by wives and daughters of the new business classes; and a creator of those fictions that would foster a cultural climate supportive of the developing American economic system.

In his criticism Howells only gradually moves toward equating "good" and "realistic" fiction, but he is careful to separate himself from the association of "realism" with immoral French prose and also careful to include "idealism" as a necessary part of good fiction. His reviews are fairly conventional, but he does repudiate aspects of popular fiction that in his eyes damage the cultural authority of the writer—heroes beyond credibility, sensational incidents, melodrama, and sentimentality. Most of his proto-Realistic comments can be found in criticism from the 1830s and 1840s: credible characters, probable motives, compositional unity. More remarkable is the relatively small number of major novels Howells reviewed. Pieces on Twain, James, Turgenev, and DeForest have been anthologized and are well known. Turgenev provided him with an important model by which fiction could be dramatic and conservative, nonpious yet not subversive. There are other reviews of fiction—by Eggleston, Aldrich, Björnson, and Cherbuliez; but more of Howells' reviews are on poetry—about which he never found an effective way to write, travel books, memoirs, and histories. *Middlemarch*, a novel he considered intellectually impressive but artistically unsuccessful, was delegated to another reviewer, as were new novels by Hardy, Trollope, Sand, and others. One cannot do everything, and he was overburdened with reviews; but some of his choices were curious and indicate a reluctance to analyze fiction not useful to him in developing his own specific paradigm: a fiction that would validate a new myth of middle-class America—dramatic but not theatrical, domestic but not sentimental, virtue-promoting but not explicitly didactic.

Meanwhile Howells' first few novels were, in part, attempts to develop for himself a mode of fictional communication with content that would be taken seriously. He begins by combining the travel book, that had a conventional credibility, with a fictional narrative and with patterns of signification for persons and places out of the romance tradition. Close study of his first two novels indicates an interplay between character drama—not yet Howells' dominant interest, landscape description, and general social commentary. The authoritative observer in this fiction implies that his generalizations grow empirically from representative observations, when in truth they determine selection of observations and character behavior. His social commentary, moreover, restricts readings that otherwise ambiguous narrative scenes might allow. A good bit of the commentary revolves around gender roles and is also connected to patterns of power and control. In these passages Howells at times connects the domestic or personal conflicts of his stories to social and political issues not manifest in the narrative itself and thereby authorizes and suggests wider readings of the narrative. The extent to which, for example, a reader extends the implications of a Kitty Ellison, a Florida Vervain, or a Lydia Blood to "the West," "America," or "innocence" depends on the nature of the apparently digressive "essays."

The marriage question is of special importance in Howells' fiction. Usually connected by scholars to traditions of the comic drama and the English novel he knew so well, it is also invariably tied to questions of power and control. Howells uses no male protagonists in his early fiction until Bartley Hubbard (Basil March in *Their Wedding Journey* is a writer-observer more than a protagonist). The women at the center are richer signifiers than Howells criticism generally suggests. Accepting his own statements on Realism, but neglecting his statements on characters as typifiers and eschewing allegorical readings of Realistic fiction, some critics neglect the metaphoric and metonymic connections Howells draws between his characters and such values as freedom, sexuality, purity, ambition, and America. In each case marriage is the potential conclusion: either a male protector is there to rescue and guard the female (and perhaps the corresponding value) or for good reasons the courtship is terminated (as with Kitty Ellison and Belle Farrell). In addition to the fundamental sexual fantasy translated in these fictions, other cultural values are articulated by relationships of protection and control, and these reinforce the "Realism" of the texts to validate a function for the writer-observer.

Howells' two strong novels *A Modern Instance* and *The Rise of Silas Lapham* authorize complexly ambivalent readings throughout, perhaps the only times Howells opened himself up to profoundly upsetting questions about his own life, contemporary America, and authorship. *A Modern Instance* was so upsetting that it led to a nervous breakdown and unsteady composition of the final chapters. In *Silas Lapham* he reasserts Howellsian control but not without a series of mixed messages that justify more variant readings than any of his other novels. With the adoption of Tolstoy as a new spiritual-aesthetic model, Howells resumed an authorial pose that could accommodate his criticism of capitalism without subversion of the social order and that could restore clarity of fictional messages if hardly stabilizing his psyche. Never was a man more in search of a Tolstoy than was Howells in the 1880s. His split from the *Atlantic*, partly over a business matter and partly out of a need for more freedom and time, coincided with a changing sense of the actual role of editors and writers. The politics of the Blaine years, moreover, severely tested his r(R)epublican myth. He defended the Republican Party and even the corrupt Blaine, refused to be a Mugwump like Twain, and never considered becoming a Democrat, for that Party was associated with everything Other for Howells. Christian Socialism provided him a way out of his political dilemma—a model of non-violent opposition to capitalism, for which he had no intrinsic love, without requiring more than an abstract acknowledgment of labor as an undifferentiated mass. Employing the language of progress, Howells could actually retreat. He effaces class problems rather than recognize class conflicts and their consequences. Like Bellamy he desires a world in which the problems are solved but finds it hard to address the process or drama of solution. He tries to emulate Tolstoy's identification with peasants, but keeps working-class immigrants at arm's length.

On the other hand Howells courageously defended Haymarket anarchists, criticized American imperialism, and was an admirable and humane man. One of few Americans identified as a serious writer who tried to address major social problems over a long career, he wanted to be involved in the flow of history, to help bring about positive change. His radicalism never quite went beyond a social-gospel utopianism without the gospel. He developed a series of artist-figures and observers as facilitators of change yet not directly involved in change, except that he then created a set of parental failures—in books like *A Hazard of New Fortunes*, *The Quality of Mercy*, and *The Landlord at Lion's Head*—whose failures necessitated a course of action for the artist-observer.

In the latter parts of his career Howells did a good bit of autobiographical writing. Unlike Twain he did not use (until very late) his boyhood experience in the West for fiction. When he turned to that period it was to develop an implicit self-myth of the American writer, a tradition of the American writer that includes Howells. *A Boy's Town, My Year in a Log Cabin,* and the more important *Years of My Youth* have elements of the Horatio Alger pattern or Carnegie pattern. But whereas the capitalist entrepreneur can validate his experience by dismissing history, by originating a new world, Howells as writer must incorporate himself within an honored tradition. *Literary Friends and Acquaintances,* a graciously genteel or impossibly saccharine set of essays on American writers (depending on one's taste) does just that, and the earlier *My Literary Passions* provides a fuller, more cosmopolitan, frame for Howells and "American Realism." The contrast with Twain is as sharp as in the 1870s. Whereas Twain the performer-promoter centers his fictive "I" and suggests meaning for himself and America through his own actions, Howells centers such contexts as family and other writers, and makes the implicit significance of his own career emerge by indirection. As he was writing these final works, of course, he was losing any authority he once had and was soon to be dismissed as a genteel conservative irrelevant to writers of the next generation.

Twain meanwhile, as complexly concerned and baffled by social changes in America, had not worked in a representational mode but had exploited the grotesque, the tall tale, the hoax, and the fable. Where Howells developed confidence between writer and reader, Twain like Melville exploited and explored author-reader relationships. Yet each wrote against a set of common forms in order to reestablish a position of authority for the writer. Almost from the beginning Twain worked in the genre of travel writing. The early letters from Hawaii, the travels with Mr. Brown to New York, the letters from Europe and the Holy Land—in conjunction with a number of early sketches—show Twain developing a voice that can leave a reader with a flexible text but one in which the author's point can be hard to pin down. In *Roughing It* he sets up a number of conventions of the initiation story and the travel book and proceeds to undermine and play variations on them; and the book moves in the middle from a young man's quest for wealth on the frontier to a decision to be a writer. In the meantime he has put on a series of virtuoso performances, connected performance thematically to power, and finally to the power of the writer. Most of the rest of Twain's books in some way revolve around patterns of performance, power (political, religious, royal, divine, Satanic, authorial), and language, and are self-reflexive in their concern for their own texts—the act of the unlettered Huck penning a sophisticated verbal fiction, the manuscripts accounting for Hank Morgan and Joan of Arc surviving centuries—or with some piece of writing or fingerprint—as in "The Man That Corrupted Hadleyburg" and *Pudd'nhead Wilson*.

A *Connecticut Yankee* is perhaps Twain's most extended commentary on power. It seems to insist on a figurative reading without clarifying its own code. To some it can be about the old (feudalism, superstition, aristocracy) and the new (science, progress, democracy). To others it can be about England and America. To still others it can be about problems of modern America, albeit with traces of a series of other projects Twain had had along the way as well as diverse influences. Hank Morgan is also a troublesome narrator, speaking for Twain along the way and yet distanced by means of a series of ironic devices. Hank is the voice of our "sensible man's guide to silly and cruel customs"; yet at times Hank seems to get more and more like his opponents—as thirsty for power as aristocrats, as capable of charlatanism as Merlin, as murderous as Morgan le Fay and other villains of the piece. In a way, perhaps, Twain takes revenge on the reader again, as James Cox says he does in *Huckleberry Finn*, by undermining the reader's sentimental rewriting of Hank as a model of benevolent progress. Had the apocalyptic ending not been drafted at the very beginning, it might seem an ironic counterpoint to Bellamy's model of peaceful change in *Looking Backward* and Donnelly's (later) *Caesar's Column*, in which disaster grows out of class rebellion rather than out of progressive change itself.

Twain has a better sense of the dynamics of power than does either Howells or Bellamy, but remarkably in a book with such insightful satire there is little sense of the relationship between power and money. There is a stock market, more like an arcade game than a nexus of power; there is a debate over tariff policy; and there are other comments connected to the money supply. In Arthurian England, of course, money was not the key to power; but it is intriguing that at a time when in his personal life Twain was obsessed with business, money, lawsuits, inventions, and bad investments, he connects power in this book to the Church. Now although churches in Twain's day had some influence as purveyors of values, they were hardly independent centers of power. While the Church certainly does not represent capitalism in this novel, neither does it play a part in the narrative or dramatic action on the book; yet it is called up as a source of evil or cruelty whenever something bad happens and is blamed for many of the wrongs in the book. The Interdict that leads to the apocalypse seems as gratuitous as the last-minute rescue of Hank and Arthur from the hangman; and in a sense it is simply a way of saying that, no, Hank's reforms cannot survive. His book, however, can—for at least thirteen centuries.

2

"A Heart of Ideality in My Realism": Howells' Early Criticism

> We would rather Winny would not read such ex-
> cruciating novels as Jane Eyre. If you could get
> her Jane Austen's stories, or Miss Mulock's out of
> the library, we should be very glad. And for my
> own part, I wish she would read biography, his-
> tory and poetry, rather than any sort of novels.[1]

In 1877 the father of American Realistic fiction advised his 14-year-old daughter not to read most novels, perhaps *Emma* but not *Jane Eyre* or other fiction of interest to teenage girls. History, biography, and poetry were more trustworthy instruments of education. Howells himself had started as a poet, and even his first two novels were governed in part by conventions from the travel book. Only with Turgenev's dramatic realism did he find in fiction itself a usable model for his own novels. By 1877, however, he had reviewed many novels for *Atlantic Monthly*, had praised some, and had implied fiction was a mode of discourse to be taken seriously, both as art and as moral communication having a significant effect on readers' behavior.

Howells was constantly writing review notices as part of his editorial work, but once said he suspected no one read them.[2] They were a chore, often done perfunctorily, but at times providing him a heuristic device for working out ideas about literature and society. When this early criticism is discussed, it is selectively used as proto-Realistic evidence for the kind of confident aesthetic Howells articulates in *Criticism and Fiction* (1891).[3] American Realism, however, is a frame created by modern academics partly around statements of the later Howells, and may distort perception of some of his earlier writings. The gospel of Realism in America, in fact, was drafted by Howells not when Realism was in the ascendant but when it was being challenged by Naturalism and other neo-Romantic modes.

A closer study of Howells' reviews and articles while at *Atlantic Monthly* reveals an editor-critic as concerned with the didactic as with the representational, interested in new authors and new literary ideas but not reviewing many strong new English novels, writing reviews of poetry based on very traditional notions of poetry, and articulating consensus Republican political attitudes. His political and literary ideas, moreover, were connected, for to a certain extent his fiction and criticism validated the social and economic changes taking place in America, justified a new American middle class, and helped create a new myth of American progress—one that replaced, in part, Whitman's more cosmic, more Emersonian myth of America's special destiny.

An ambitious young Westerner, Howells used his training in printing and journalism to achieve the success in literature—if not the money— that Vanderbilt and Carnegie were achieving in railroads and steel. Identifying with the paradigm of the self-made man, he wrote that Horace Greeley's memoirs were about Greeley's rise from struggling boyhood— "a perpetual romance; it delights and touches all, for in this nation it is in some degree the story of every man's life or the vision of his desires" (*Atlantic* 23:260).[4] Howells and Twain, in fact, were the first two serious American prose writers to set out to make it as professionals on this entrepreneurial model and to succeed.[5] One major problem both faced was the lack of authority held by writers and writing in an America of shopkeepers, engineers, industrialists, and pioneers. In different ways each writer developed strategies to establish that authority.[6]

Outside of his novels, Howells' primary strategy was his editorial leadership of *Atlantic Monthly*. Through his selection of material and the influence of his own reviews, he tried to alter the discourse about literature so as to increase its significance and to solidify his own position as the spokesman for what was new, a position independent of the older Fields-Lowell-Holmes group that had established *Atlantic Monthly*.[7] He brought new ideas to literary discussion, though they emerge more in criticisms directed against romantic conventions than in clear positions on what literature should be. On poetry he had few interesting ideas. His most common criticism of new poets was that they were often obscure.[8] To Walt Whitman's sensuous lines he never reconciled himself, and in general he relied on the strictures of traditional metrics and versification to evaluate new works.

Howells' reactions to Whitman's poetry provide an instructive context for reading his paradigm of a new American fiction. Whitman's democratic, dionysiac sensualism was, to Howells' mind, disruptive and tasteless, a threat to the design according to which he saw America moving ahead. Howells' distaste for *Leaves of Grass* appeared as early as

1860. In a May 21 review in the *Ohio State Journal* he called Whitman's verse "utterly bamboozling," giving readers the "unpleasant doubt whether the author is sublime or a beast, with an inclination toward the latter belief." The portrait included in the book correspondingly was "that of a man-about-horses—slouch, insolent, cute, coarse." Soon thereafter he was off to New England, to the laying on of hands by Lowell and Holmes, and having nothing to do with Whitman's barbaric yawp and city-streets democracy, though a bit fearful that Whitman might become "the fashion" and that everyone might start wearing "Walt Whitman hats." Two months earlier (March 24) in the same newspaper he had sarcastically responded to Emerson's claim that *Leaves of Grass* was the "representative book of poetry of our age." To the young Howells it was "lawless, measureless, rhythmless and miserable." Whitman was in error in discarding old "forms and laws," without which a poet cannot reach "the reader's heart through his bewildered understanding."[9] In discussing poetry, Howells was confused by apparent obscurities, upset by original poetics, and put off by a diction and a sensuality that did not mesh well with his own social and political values. In fiction, however, he criticized the histrionics, melodrama, and sentimentality whose vogue threatened the writer's authority in an age of empiricism and social science. Although he did not review strong new novels by Eliot, Meredith, and Hardy, his reviews of Turgenev and Björnson were insightful and incisive, and brought the Russian and the Scandinavian their first serious attention in America.[10] Howells regularly brought new work by Twain before American audiences, printed James's fiction in *Atlantic Monthly*, and wrote reviews of *A Passionate Pilgrim* and *Nathaniel Hawthorne*.

He also published in 1882 a controversial article for *Century* praising James at the expense of Dickens and Thackeray. As he was establishing his own position among New England literati, and being the self-conscious western outsider, Howells seems to have still feared English domination of American writing. Negative comments on such authors as Trollope, Bulwer, and Thackeray, as well as a more developed attack on Dickens, suggest this concern. Howells criticized Dickens largely through comments on a biography by John Forster, who Howells said was taken in by the Dickens myth and lacked critical insight. In his days at the *Nation*, Howells had satirized Josiah Holland, influential editor of *Scribner's* and popular author of sentimental literature. Not only did Holland have the status within letters that Howells sought but also his kind of writing was exactly the sort of thing undermining the cultural authority of writers. Though competition and hostility between the two continued until a deathbed reconciliation, Howells did not again discuss or publicize Holland's work.[11] He went after bigger game, and denigrated Dickens' bewitching "popular romances" that beguile mass audiences "to laughter or tears." Dickens' success was a mere "actor's success," based on exploiting audiences with melodramatic tricks and sentimentality (*Atlantic* 29:239-41). Earlier Howells had displayed no antipathy towards Dickens, but had enjoyed his readings and even dinners with him.[12] He disagreed with some of Dickens' criticisms of America, but they did not arouse his hostility. At some point between 1868 and 1872, however, around the time of Dickens' death, he decided that Dickens' fiction represented an unhealthy fashion that had to be replaced. At the same time, curiously, he discovered Mark Twain, an America writer somewhat like Dickens. While criticizing Dickens for "an actor's success," he did not mention that Twain's success was also an actor's success, that he thrived on performance and audience control, in both personal readings and written texts.

Twain and DeForest were, with Henry James, the new American writers Howells puffed most energetically. Except for casual praise of the poetry of Longfellow and Lowell, he rarely discussed the work of American writers preceding his own generation, at least until such later retrospective works as *Literary Friends and Acquaintance*. For Howells at this time, Washington Irving had been the best early American writer. Although Howells' fiction, for example *A Foregone Conclusion* and *The Undiscovered Country*, reveals his concern with Hawthorne as a strong predecessor, he did not in his published criticism come to terms with Hawthorne as James did. Nor, although he energetically sought new American talent, did he explicitly concern himself at this stage with American literary nationalism or the great American novel. The Civil War had made Americans temporarily more cautious about the oratory of national destiny. On the other hand, Howells' critical essays on Italian literature for *North American Review* cover Italian literary nationalism and may have provided him a means for working through a critical problem for which he lacked perspective and distance when confronting American texts.

Howells did, however, offer two different predictions for the new American novel. Once he wrote that the story of a representative young man's development, specifically Thomas Bailey Aldrich's *Story of a Bad Boy*, provided a paradigm that for Howells was "a new thing in ... American literature" (*Atlantic* 25:124).[13] The "life of an American boy" representing "the great average of boys" was an original conception that would "give us the American novel," and certainly fit in with the suggestion he made in reviewing Greeley's autobiography that the rise from "struggling boyhood" was *the* American paradigm. All this mixed strangely with denigration of the author of *Oliver Twist*, *Nicholas Nickleby*, *David Copperfield*, and *Great Expectations*. The second model was the picaresque. In discussing Ralph Keeler's *Vagabond Adventures*, Howells argued that "the truly American novel, when it comes to be written, will be a story of personal adventure after the fashion of Gil Blas, and many of the earlier English fictions" (*Atlantic* 26:759). Howells wrote neither stories of bad boys nor picaresque adventures—Twain did—but at this point he was composing *Their Wedding Journey* and was concerned with combining the advantages of fictional flexibility and travel-book authority.

Not only was he interested in dealing with an America now continental in scope, but also he was interested in achieving credibility for fictional communication. Sentimental romances lacked that, as did any fiction based on sensational turns of plot that had no reference to experience. Similarly Dickens' performances had but fleeting authority over ingenuous audiences. Howells said that he had contempt for current audiences ("I rather despise existing readers") and that a writer like James would have to educate and create his own audience as he went along.[14] In fact, he found that "generally the literary world is dull," and gradually he saw the need to establish a new path in prose in order to achieve his goals.[15]

Thus the emergence of his first proto-Realist comments. His early interest in verisimilitude, however, was in authenticity of signifiers—that is, the material of ordinary life—not in the process of mediation. He did not particularly demean symbolism or allegory or figurative modes in general, which to some scholars are part of Romanticism. There was no sense of difference between on the one hand a developed "realistic" character being representative of a category of persons and on the other hand a developed character suggesting a quality or a region or a value. His own early fiction, in fact, has characters that invite semi-allegorical interpretations; but that general issue was not his concern in these reviews.

His interest in the use of ordinary experience relates to his desire for authority: that which can be observed is validated. It also echoes Wordsworth's and Emerson's notion of the truest significance emerging from ordinary experience. Howells generally defined what he admired against the shortcomings of conventional literature. Certain well drawn fictional characters, for example, were "so unlike characters in novels as to be like people in life" (*Atlantic* 20:121). Björnson was effective largely because he presented lives of men and women honestly without the "surprising incident or advantageous circumstance" on which popular fiction depends (*Atlantic* 25:512).[16] Howells always emphasized "character," but it was not always clear what "character" meant. In his early novels he tested the signification of characters through social themes and through geographical and topical symbolism. In an early review, of Bayard Taylor's *Kennett Square*, he wrote that unlike Taylor he himself was not concerned that fictional characters be based on particular real people (*Atlantic* 17:777).[17] Elsewhere, however, he praised characters that were "faithful studies of American life" (*Atlantic* 29:362-64) or "true to nature" like "our friends and neighbors" (*Atlantic* 22:634). In his 1882 article on James, Howells argued that the novelist's main business was "to possess his reader with a due conception of his characters and the situations in which they find themselves."[18]

At that point in his career he was balanced between a growing psychological interest and a more traditional ethical interest, in which for all the talk of close observation of local reality, characters were still tokens of certain values. The trauma over *A Modern Instance* was in a sense Howells' crisis over this conflict in characterization, though the crisis started as early as *The Undiscovered Country* (1880). In *A Modern Instance* what begins as a romance of geographical signification like some of Howells' earlier fiction—here, the transient young male, the New England girl, the move to the city—becomes a profoundly though not literally autobiographical study of personal disintegration. The weakness of the ending derived in part from Howells' attempt through the Hallecks to reestablish and retreat to a kind of allegorical signification.

In his early criticism, however, reservations about "realism"—still a pejorative term in genteel circles—were more frequent than arguments for realism. Fiction should not be intolerably preachy like Henry Ward Beecher's *Norwood* but should instruct. "A book has no business to be merely literature," he wrote in 1870, but should "disenchant youth" and illustrate grief and poverty in their "true colors" (*Atlantic* 26:759). Apparently America for this unmellowed Howells was not governed by "smiling aspects" of life, for he said "the only condition of making life like ours tolerable in literature is to paint it exactly as it is" (*Atlantic* 26:760). On the other hand, "mere allegiance to the facts of everyday life" for their own sake was a low goal for literature, for, as he wrote to E. C. Stedman in 1878, though "I am devotedly a realist ... I hope I keep always a heart of ideality in my realism."[19] A novel "must mean something" and "show that I had felt strongly about it," he wrote to James Osgood in 1881, echoing a comment three years earlier to T. W. Higginson that "I should be ashamed and sorry if my novels did not unmistakably teach a lenient, generous, and liberal life."[20] There may be a difference between an obligation to show poverty in true colors and a commitment to teach a liberal view of life, but in all these cases lies a notion of the moral purpose of the novel, and it rested on the credibility derived from professional observation and ordering of ordinary experience.

Although Howells praised Zola's fiction, he generally disdained "French realism," for example, Daudet's *Numa*: bad art comes from "the bad French morality."[21] He argued once that characters should be exemplary.[22] One problem with Dickens and Thackeray was that their characters were not, and "lady novelists" were notorious for making vice attractive. One problem with sensational romances was their tendency to make murderers heroes and immoral women heroines (*Atlantic* 25:247-48). The other major problem was that reliance on plot, adventure, and incident to provide thrills in fiction—"the world has outgrown that need"—destroyed the author's credibility as an observer of human nature (*Atlantic* 25:633-34). The decline of Bulwer and Scott was for Howells the surest sign of aesthetic progress among American readers, whereas a lingering taste for Scott was a sign of the South's backwardness.[23]

The distinction between "novel" and "romance" was crucial very early to Howells' definition of fiction and its purposes. He criticized James for not more clearly distinguishing between the two. Although by 1886 he could speak more belligerently of "banging the babes of romance about," once he had maintained a sympathetic if condescending attitude toward romances that were neither of the sensational-sentimental variety nor of the historical-extravaganza kind. Sylvester Judd's saccharine romance *Margaret* was in 1871 still, to Howells' taste, comparable to the fiction of Goethe and Hawthorne and better "than the best new novel of our generation" (*Atlantic* 27:144).[24] In 1869 he appreciated Viktor Rydberg's *The Last Athenian*, a historical romance of fourth-century Athens. Only later did he turn against historical fiction on the grounds that a novelist cannot have observed such people and so cannot depict them accurately. Taylor's *Kennett Square*, he said, actually achieved its strength from the distance Taylor had on characters set in the past.

The ideal aspects of romance were like those of the novel, but lacked their epistemological validity. Romance subordinated character to landscape, with meaning emerging from setting. Romance need not adhere to "strict rules of probability" but only internal coherence (*Atlantic* 31:105). False endings, failures of composition, inconsistency in attitude elicited from readers were flaws in both forms; but the novelist's calling in Howells' day was clearly a more serious *business*. Howells wrote to his father in 1881, "I know rather more about the business of writing novels than any critic living."[25] He was very much the writer as businessman, and, despite his attacks on commercialism, carved out a career only possible in an age of business.

Such an option was not quite available a generation earlier when Hawthorne and Poe struggled for a hearing. As the one generally accepted strong predecessor in American fiction, of course, Hawthorne was someone with whom nearly every serious new American writer had to come to grips. Whereas James, however, worked through that relationship in both his fiction and a monograph on Hawthorne, Howells adopted a model of literary evolution in which, whatever the virtues of earlier writers, contemporary writers could advance beyond them. Hawthorne thereby became an "innocent" with a "life of high purposes." Five years earlier Howells, in praising Thomas Bailey Aldrich's *Prudence Palfrey*, had commented that the romance was all a New England writer could do, for a New England novel was not really possible (*Atlantic* 34:228-29). It had too narrow a civilization "for the dramatic realism" that to Howells, now a full convert to Turgenev's method, was essential for the novel. Writers like Hawthorne, Hale, and Holmes had to resort to immaterizalizing facts, allegory, symbolism, or psychological case studies. At the same time he could describe the South of 1840, with its range of rich planters, yeoman farmers, poor crackers, and slaves as apt for novel-writing, and speculated we would never again "see a phase of civilization so apt for the novelist's purposes" (*Atlantic* 34:362).

For many Northerners, the South continued to be a convenient scapegoat. Families who had lost sons in battle, intellectuals like Emerson who had lost myths, politicians who could gain votes by "waving the bloody shirt," and businessmen who could profit from Reconstruction— all found the South an object for exploitation. At first Howells wished greater punishment for Jefferson Davis and Confederate leaders (*Atlantic* 23:261).[26] Assailing the Southern character as naturally violent and infe- rior, he sarcastically concluded that Southerners had been created "with some important differences from other men," with a nature "inverted" so as to believe slavery a positive good (*Atlantic* 23:517). Ridiculing the dearth of good writing in the South, he ironically said that Southerners had "not only a lost cause, but a lost literature to lament" (*Atlantic* 23:515). Books such as Raphael Semmes' *Memoirs of Service Afloat during the War Between the States*, a self-pitying apology, would abuse the minds of young people: they would see themselves as gentle blood and not learn American virtues of enterprise and thrift (*Atlantic* 23:515- 18; 24:124-28). Howells preferred books such as Whitelaw Reid's *Ohio in the War* that showed little sympathy for the South (*Atlantic* 21:252-54).

By the early 1870s he had changed. In his 1869 review of Higgin- son's *Army Life in a Black Regiment*, he noted that the national mind was more concerned with injustice to Chinese than oppression of Negroes, for Americans are changeable, like "a woman's mind" as he put it. Though Higginson's portrayal of his "simple childlike warriors" was appealing, Howells doubted it would re-ignite a new concern for freedmen (*Atlantic* 24:643-44). Despite an abolitionist background, Howells like most white Americans had little taste for integration or amalgamation. In a review of a travel book on Brazil by Louis Agassiz and his wife, Howells recounted without comment arguments on the evils of mixing races and on the necessity for racial purity (*Atlantic* 21:383-84). When Albert Pike's *The Prostrate South* appeared in 1874, with its account of Reconstruction government in South Carolina, Howells uncritically accepted Pike's case (*Atlantic* 33:233-34). A "sable despotism" of former slaves, illiterate and unfit to make laws, fit only to steal money as Pike said, was taxing whites out of the state and destroying South Carolina. Howells did not doubt the truth since "facts and figures" were so plentiful. A critic generally quick to question assumptions and arguments in books he reviewed here showed less desire to address racial issues than to restore inter-sectional harmony.

Howells was never the enthusiastic Southern recruiter that Richard Watson Gilder was for *Scribner's*, and he preferred to support mountain-area Southerners such as Mary Murfree rather than plantation-area writers such as Thomas Nelson Page. Moreover, he could support Pike's book but not Semmes's because Pike did not explicitly defend slavery. That was taboo. The bloody war, the Republican Party, American myths—all for Howells depended on the wrongness of slavery. In a curious encomium for Lowell's war poetry, he asserted that "since the great moral revolt against slavery began to ennoble our politics," literature had played a major role in moral and political discourse, as if the very origin of a morally serious literature were inseparable from the issue that defined America in its greatest crisis (*Atlantic* 39:93). Even as in 1876 and 1877 he was admitting that *Uncle Tom's Cabin* no longer had for him the impact it had during slavery, he was also, in a review of Harriet Martineau's autobiography, remarking that "the Americans of thirty years ago were ... corrupted by the fear and favor of slavery," the perverse belief that slavery was right (*Atlantic* 39:626).[27]

If the compromises of the 1870s left Howells assured that the blot of slavery was gone, he could be a bit more nostalgic about Southern culture.[28] *Kate Beaumont*, a novel by DeForest about ante-bellum South Carolina, provided, he said, "the first full and perfect picture of Southern society of the times before the war" (*Atlantic* 29:362-65). Such a sympathetic portrayal by, according to Howells, America's best current novelist, and a Union veteran to boot, may have contributed to Howells' new sentiment. Of course, DeForest in his book did play down the slavery issue in order to represent a set of Southern characters with as much sympathy as he could muster. Two years later, in another review, Howells attacked slavery and dismissed aristocratic virtues and graces as having social costs too great for society at large, but nostalgically lamented the lost combination of magnanimity, courage, openhandedness, and stately grace found in Kentucky gentlemen (*Atlantic* 34:30).[29]

A favorable reception for *A Chance Acquaintance* was important because, he felt, it showed his sympathy with the spirit of democracy.[30] He opposed the new railroad plutocrats as he had Southern slaveowners, and could pose as one who no longer had to blame the rich but could "pity them."[31] Like Twain, however, he indulged in anti-Irish sneers and felt that a suffrage limited by education would be healthy for democracy (*Atlantic* 34:111). Like Twain he also had contempt for the popular image of the Native American as a Noble Savage, and praised Francis Parkman for helping us to "desentimentalize" the loss of "uninteresting races" (*Atlantic* 25:123).

Howells' attitudes are typical of Liberal Republicanism, of the readers he sought and addressed, of the class whose experience his fiction validated. The model and the myth, however, began to collapse in the

1880s. The replacement of self-made industrialists by impersonal combinations of finance capitalism, the succession of James G. Blaine and all he represented to an authority once held by friends and relations like Hayes and Garfield—to say nothing of Lincoln, the increasing self-doubts and literary skepticism developed at the time of *A Modern Instance*, the reading of Tolstoy and the frustrations of the Haymarket affair, all left Howells sadder and wiser. What ensued, however, was not a shift to Democratic populism or the cause of labor. Howells' sympathetic review of John Hay's popular, anonymously published *The Breadwinners* seems a bit disingenuous but was not really insincere. Minimizing the strongly anti-union sub-text of the novel, Howells argued that Hay had no prejudice against workingmen, that he did not criticize strikers until they burned and pillaged property.[32] Howells supported strikes, but would himself call out troops if life and property were threatened.[33] He smugly concluded that "we are all workingmen" in America, or "sons of workingmen." The "idle rich" (gambling speculators) and "idle poor" are most to be dreaded, not the working rich and poor.

When in the late 1880s and 1890s Howells came to sympathize with working-class persons and causes, and to recognize the alienation of labor, his new vision was one in which peaceful collectivist reform, with the writer-observer as catalyst, was not only possible but might be a self-fulfilling prophecy. Eschewing the apocalyptic jeremiads of Donnelly and Twain, Howells killed off such symbols of confrontation as Reverend Peck and Berthold Lindau. During these same years Howells was an aggressive spokesman for his program of American Realism. Analysis of his social essays and literary articles of this period is a project for another time; but three observations connect Howells' writing at this time with his scattered, unsystematic social and literary comments of the 1870s. First, the pattern of furious enlightened confrontation with social issues in conjunction with establishment of professional credibility, followed by a retreat to less controversial projects, is the same pattern enacted by such reformist social scientists as Richard Ely, Samuel Bemis, Henry Carter Adams, and Edward Ross. Ambitious young professionals, they met institutional opposition to their advocacy of regulation of business or the money supply, and after a flurry of conflict reestablished themselves in a safer position.[34] They had to divorce their function as trained observer-analyst from their function as participant-citizen. In all modes of serious verbal discourse, a market economy which commodified work and professional participation could allow for few successful marriages of the two functions.[35]

Second, the program of American Realism, outlined in *Criticism and Fiction* and elaborated in other reviews and articles, became for him a system that could cloak the conflicts and discontinuities of American experience with an evolutionary myth. As America could be for Whitman,

Realism for Howells could be the high arc of the projectile of western culture. Whatever threats and injustices continued, Realism with its fusion of representative depiction and tolerant liberal idealism would help guide America aright. James was more conscious of the writer's inconsistent position, of the gap between the modern writer's representational and participatory functions. But Howells had an aesthetic within which he could satisfyingly explain and support the broad range of authors he reviewed after 1885, and within which he could counter both naturalism and myopic romanticism.

Finally, the autobiographical fabric he wove during his last thirty years did three important things for Howells. It implicitly positioned him within a great tradition, and revised a literary history that could lead up to Howells and American Realism. It justified his career along lines he had drawn in reviewing Greeley's autobiography, the success story of a diligent, hard-working poor boy, but also made him a special, because a literary, example of the pattern. It established a standard of reference in the individual life not in a larger social world. It is curious that the generation of writers who made the "I" their subject—Emerson, Thoreau, Melville, Whitman—did not write autobiographies, but their followers in the Age of Realism—Clemens, Howells, James, Adams—all did write autobiographies. The age as it were required a justification, a "pertinent … account" Thoreau might have said, of captains of industry and robber barons. More to the point it also provided them a ready audience for turning their experience into exempla that would not only rationalize their performance but would assure its effects by making it a model for subsequent generations.[36]

Notes

1. W. D. Howells, *Selected Letters*, ed. G. Arms and C. K. Lohmann (Boston: Twayne, 1979) 2:157.

2. W. D. Howells, *Selected Letters*, ed. G. Arms *et al.* (Boston: Twayne, 1979) 1:348.

3. The most useful anthologies of criticism by Howells are *W. D. Howells as Critic*, ed. Edwin H. Cady (London: Routledge & Kegan Paul, 1973), and *Criticism and Fiction and Other Essays*, ed. C. M. Kirk and R. Kirk (New York: New York UP, 1959). Several dissertations have discussed Howells' early criticism. Of particular note are Elizabeth B. Stanton, "William Dean Howells: A Study of His Literary Theories and Practices During His *Atlantic Monthly* Years, 1866-1881" (Ohio State Univ., 1942); Robert E. Butler, "William Dean Howells as Editor of the *Atlantic*

Monthly" (Rutgers Univ., 1950); and Howard K. Moore, "William Dean Howells as a Literary Critic" (Boston Univ., 1950).

4. My primary bibliographical sources for Howells' reviews are William M. Gibson and George Arms, *A Bibliography of William Dean Howells* (New York: Arno, 1948), and the *Atlantic Index*.

5. Longfellow had succeeded, in one sense, as a poet for a new audience, but did so by forfeiting originality and authority to accommodate himself to the new audience, trying to "fill the little interludes of life." Hawthorne sought the kind of success and authority Howells and Clemens later achieved, but conditions for it were not yet possible. Irving and Cooper achieved some popularity, success, and respect, but more from the position of literary gentlemen not performers and entrepreneurs.

6. For background on this matter, see Emory Elliott, *Revolutionary Writers: Literature and Authority in the New Republic, 1725-1810* (New York: Oxford UP, 1982); and Eric Sundquist, *Home as Found: Authority and Genealogy in Nineteenth-century American Literature* (Baltimore: Johns Hopkins UP, 1979).

7. For a slightly different perspective on Howells at the *Atlantic Monthly*, see *Fields of the Atlantic Monthly: Letters to an Editor, 1861-1870*, ed. James C. Austin (San Marino: Huntington Library, 1953).

8. See, for example, the review of Rossetti in the July 1870 *Atlantic Monthly* or the review of Browning in July 1873.

9. A letter to Lowell in 1865 suggested Whitman was not refined enough for American poetry. In 1866 Howells expressed exasperation at "the whole Whitman business" (*Selected Letters* 1:271). A review of John O'Connor's book on Whitman was critical of the poet (*Round Table* 20 January 1866: 36-37). The previous year Howells called *Drum Taps* "unspeakably inartistic" and said it "does not give you sensation in a portable shape" (*Round Table* 11 November 1865: 147-48). We do not want, Howells said, to be partners with the poet, but to seek poetry's effect. "The people fairly rejected" Whitman's work, and those who did not "were readers with a cultivated taste for the outlandish."

10. The review of *Middlemarch* (April 1873) by A. G. Sedgwick was sensitive and probing. Howells more than once reviewed Eliot's poetry and said it was not as good as her fiction, but he never discussed her fiction at length. He seems to have enjoyed *Romola* more than *Middlemarch* (*Selected Letters* 1:175 and 3:23), despite his admiration for Eliot's "intellectual achievement" in the latter.

11. For discussions of the Holland incident, see the two basic biographies: Edwin H. Cady, *The Road to Realism* (Syracuse: Syracuse UP, 1956); and Kenneth S. Lynn, *William Dean Howells: An American Life* (New York: Harcourt Brace Jovanovich, 1971).

12. Cady, *The Road to Realism* 48, 51 and *Selected Letters* 1:287-88, 292-94.

13. See the discussion of the "boy-book" in Edwin Cady, *The Light of Common Day* (Bloomington: Indiana UP, 1971) 96-101.

14. *Selected Letters* 1:283: to Charles Eliot Norton in 1867.

15. *Selected Letters* 1:352: to Henry James in 1870.

16. Howells complained that contemporary fiction seemed to have "no middle ground between magnificent drawing-rooms and the most un-pleasant back-alleys, or between very refined and well-born company and the worst reprobates."

17. Actually Howells addressed this issue as early as 12 April 1860 (*Ohio State Journal*), when he wrote that artistically "it does not seem to be best to make characters ... too much like actualities ..., for what the ... character gains in depth and intensity, it loses in that breadth and uni-versality which makes the personages of Shakespeare real men and women." Howells also questioned the ethics of such use of real figures, especially applying a new trait "to the formation of a character" that might be recognized as a likeness of the real person, and having him then behave in a way that the original would not. Howells was discussing Hawthorne's *The Marble Faun*.

18. *Century Magazine* 25 (November 1882): 24-29. In comparing Eliot with James, Howells said that "with George Eliot an ethical purpose is dominant, and with Mr. James an artistic purpose" (26). In describing novels of the present as superior to novels of the past, he went on to say, "The art of fiction has, in fact, become a finer art in our day than it was with Dickens and Thackeray."

19. *Selected Letters* 2:214.

20. *Selected Letters* 2:277 and 2:238.

21. W. D. Howells, *Selected Letters*, ed. R. C. Leitz III *et al.* (Boston: Twayne, 1980) 3:74-75 (letter to Hay, 30 July 1883); and 3:12-13 (letter to Hay, 18 March 1882), in which he said, "I am a great admirer of French workmanship, and I read everything of Zola's that I can lay hands on. But I have to hide the books from my children."

22. See Howells' review of Charles Reade, *A Terrible Temptation*, in *Atlantic Monthly* 28 (September 1871): 383-84.

23. Howells showed little interest in Scott's contribution to Realism, well researched realistic details to provide accuracy of setting and costume.

24. I am not offering a full re-appraisal of Howells' attitude toward the romance. Appreciation of its complexity goes back at least to Louis J.

Budd's important article, "W. D. Howells's Defence of the Romance," *PMLA* 67 (1952): 32-42. Also see Joseph H. Gardner, "Howells: The 'Realist' as Dickensian," *Modern Fiction Studies* 16 (1970): 323-43; and Seymour Gross and Rosalie Murphy, "Commonplace Reality and the Romantic Phantoms: Howells' *A Modern Instance* and *The Rise of Silas Lapham*," *Studies in American Fiction* 4 (1976): 1-14.

25. *Selected Letters* 2:296. As early as 3 November 1860 (*Ohio State Journal*), Howells attacked Lamartine for criticizing America's treatment of her writers. Howells said that American writers were not mendicants corrupted by the patronage of kings and princes, reduced to the status of court "buffoons." Instead an author can receive the "love and admiration of the people, after they have paid for his books." Arguing that American authorship had achieved a free democratic foundation, Howells asserted, "Here ... the publication of a poem or a novel (which is the modern poem) is an affair of business—between the author's agent and the public." An "enlightened criticism," moreover, places author and reader in "true relations to each other" and makes America the land which actually most esteems its authors. Howells' own post-war experience in the business world did, of course, slightly temper this youthful enthusiasm for literature's alliance with the marketplace.

26. This comment was made in the review of Greeley's memoirs.

27. Also see *Selected Letters* 2:125.

28. Howells did not deal directly in a novel with a racial issue until 1892 (*An Imperative Duty*). In that period, to be sure, he was supporting the work of Charles Chesnutt, as later he supported the work of Paul Laurence Dunbar. In those years he was relatively enlightened about racial matters, and about American imperialism.

29. Also see Howells' review of George Cary Eggleston's *A Rebel's Recollections*, *Atlantic Monthly* 35 (February 1875): 237-38.

30. *Selected Letters* 2:24.

31. *Selected Letters* 2:24 and 112.

32. *Century Magazine* 28 (May 1884): 153-54. This review, of course, was written after Howells left *Atlantic Monthly* and only two years before the Haymarket incident profoundly affected his feelings about such issues.

33. Also see *John Hay-Howells Letters*. Ed. G. Monteiro and B. Murphy (Boston: Twayne, 1980) xxii-xxiv, 60, 67-68. Howells was one of very few persons to whom Hay revealed the secret of his authorship.

34. See especially Mary O. Furner, *Advocacy and Objectivity: A Crisis in the Professionalization of American Social Science, 1865-1905*

(Lexington: U of Kentucky P, 1975); but also Thomas L. Haskell, *The Emergence of Professional Social Science* (Urbana: U Illinois P, 1977).

35. See the first chapter of Carolyn Porter, *Seeing and Being: The Plight of the Participant Observer in Emerson, James, Adams, and Faulkner* (Middletown, CT: Wesleyan UP, 1981).

36. I am indebted to David J. Nordloh for his help in using the Howells materials at Indiana University.

3

Their Wedding Journey:
In Search of a New Fiction

Their Wedding Journey was not William Dean Howells' first attempt at a novel. Nor was it his first published book, since a collection of poems, a campaign biography, two volumes on Italy, and a set of fictional sketches had all come before. It was, however, a beginning, partly because it was his first published novel and in fact his first serious book originally drafted as a book; moreover, it consciously asserted itself as a beginning.

Their Wedding Journey was also a literary manifesto in which Howells announced a new kind of fiction based on the significance of "ordinary" middle-class experience, of representative episodes and scenes from "everyday" life. The nature and extent of that significance, and signification, however, Howells at this point could only assert through devices more often associated with drama or poetry or romance— thematic patterns of imagery or motifs, and explicit association of characters with values or categories or types. At the same time he tried to establish a more authoritative mode of signification, however, he also sought a narrative voice and authorial position defined not by romantic alienation or separation from the workaday world but rather by participation in that world.[1] Finally, *Their Wedding Journey* depends on an aggressively masculine assertion of control over the female and feminine, not only through plot and narrative but through numerous gender-related asides throughout the text. While the biographical sources for this theme have been better discussed elsewhere, in this first novel it also implies that Howells saw his new mode of fiction as a way to retrieve control of the literary market from the sentimental romancers Hawthorne once called a "mob of scribbling women" as well as to reverse what Ann Douglas has more recently tagged the "feminization of American culture."

31

Hawthorne had located his romances mid-way between fairyland and reality. Howells, shifting the space of fiction towards hard fact or experience, located his novels mid-way between the romance and reality. Leaving out fantasy, he tried to navigate between experience and conventional literary forms (romance), which throughout *Their Wedding Journey* suggest fiction-making or meaning-making devices necessary to the mediation of experience into fiction.[2] Although Howells advocated the use of ordinary and credible characters and events, he did not mean his fiction merely to reflect. Rather he retained the moral voice and shaping vision he had always associated with poetry and drama.

As the travelers move from New York City, that site least imbued in this novel with romance and history, and most impressing itself as hard fact, to Quebec, the most historical and romantic site, the writer moves from a tactic of inductively asserting significance—largely through concentrated imagery of heat, dryness, and enclosure—to a tactic of peeling off layers of romantic and "historical" significance. In conveying this experience, Howells dramatizes the problematic relationship between perception, cognition, and (literary) performance. In fact, the entire surface of a happy honeymoon trip being recounted by an optimistic friend of the travelers is counterpointed against the book's skepticism toward literature. At the same time, the optimistic surface asserts a new beginning, an empirical quest, that for the writer signifies a step towards a new fiction, rather than the confident and much less interesting apology of his later *Criticism and Fiction*.

By several devices *Their Wedding Journey* sets itself against sentimental domestic romances of its own day. The newlyweds are presented as older, more mature and experienced than the usual paradigms of young love. Romantic adventures and incidents are played down, and the usual falsifications of fiction are disparaged. Howells was developing his own kind of domestic romance within the framework of the travel book, which in the nineteenth century had empirical authority, literary prestige, and a more masculine orientation than did popular fiction. A genre as protean as the novel, moreover, it might include texts as diverse as reports of explorers, such as Lewis and Clark, and symbolic journeys such as *A Week on the Concord and Merrimack Rivers*. It might take the form of a trip west defining a frontier or a trip to Europe providing perspectives on the Old World from the point of view of the New. Before Howells, works such as *Typee* and *Two Years Before the Mast* had already blurred the boundary between fiction and reality. *Typee* is in one sense a precursor of *Their Wedding Journey*. Both are fictionalized autobiographical accounts, based in part on earlier journals or published sources, that have also been read as first novels. One is first-person, the other third-person, but both through their Adamic posture use recorded experiences to comment on "America" and American values. Their styles and settings do reflect the quarter-century gap between their compositions; their moods and ideologies are substantially different; and the clear nature/culture thematic conflict at the center of *Typee* is more ambiguous in Howells' book. But beneath both texts is a similar impulse to invest the writer's personal experience with larger significance and to make that writer/experiencer represent peculiarly American traits.[3]

Their Wedding Journey makes use of a husband-wife pair of observers, perhaps influenced by George William Curtis' *Prue and I*, and establishes a thematically significant itinerary: New York, Rochester, Niagara, Montreal, Quebec, and ships and railroads along the way. The travelers go West and yet also to Europe, by association with Quebec and Montreal. Basil and Isabel never enter a truly primitive world, and for Howells the physically primitive was not crucial to modern America. Westerners were as capable of refinement as Easterners. Sentimentalization of either the primitive or the historically primeval was a source of falseness.

If he did not value Nature as the Romantics did, Howells did polemicize the value of ordinary experience as Wordsworth did, without of course a rural emphasis. Like Whitman he found significant ordinary experience in the city as well as in the country and village. If, like Whitman and Emerson, he adopted an Adamic posture, he did not find correspondence between the ordinary event and a transcendent truth, but rather connected the ordinary event to a social meaning within an empirical context. The author still spoke with moral authority; but while dropping both the trappings of popular fiction and the visionary dimension of romantic poetry, he established a self-consciously masculine, scientific pose—like the modern journalist—within which he could validate domestic virtues, the special nature of America, and the writer as the one who mediated observation into usable truth.

Their Wedding Journey opens and closes with comments on writing and the text itself, at first in relation to romance, at the end in relation to theatre. The final dialogue between Basil and Isabel is a conventional theatrical device—one Howells used in *Out of the Question*—in which the last words of the play provide the title. Basil has just advised his wife that "our travels are incommunicably our own," that it would be impossible to "make our wedding-journey theirs." Howells' message, of course, is that such experiences through fiction do become "theirs." With Isabel replying, "Who wants it ... to be Their Wedding Journey?" Howells exploits the gap between speaking and writing. As spoken by Isabel the stress is on "wants" and the question ironic. As written the question invites a neutral and open reading. Because of the shifting nature of pronouns, moreover, the Marches who are "our" in the dialogue become "their" in the title—to both narrator and reader, who becomes "our."

The ending also comes full circle with the narrator's prefatory comment that he will merely "talk of some ordinary traits of American life as these appeared to them, to speak a little of well-known and easily accessible places, to present now a bit of landscape and now a sketch of character." The purpose of fiction is defined not as tracing the unseen from the seen or drawing correspondence between the natural and spiritual, but as showing forth what often has been seen but never so well expressed.

Fiction would then signify mimetically, with models drawn from ordinary observation and with identification between reader and protagonist. Basil, "like a true American, like you," shrinks from asserting himself. He and Isabel pretend not to be newlyweds (4, 18, 64) and certainly not "ordinary" (63). Their own vanity is undercut in scenes in Rochester. A waiter does not know from their appearance that they are from Boston. They like others "have the depravity to smile" at the misfortunes of a German immigrant who does not know the conventions of railroad merchants. They slash their friends the Ellisons "to pieces" when that couple are absent, and display a doubtful morality smuggling at the border. They are ironically described as having all the venal sins of ordinary people—readers included—but are romanticized by the end as a new kind of American and literary norm.

Howells resorts to self-conscious apologies for the potential dullness of his material. "True" art and "sincere" observation are "more worthy to be studied" than the heroic and, he pretends, more amusing. In his "feeble thoughts" and "dumb, stupid desires" and "obtuse selfishness" man is most entertaining (55). Since "want of incident" and "barren details with their life-like weariness" (60) are most typical of life, they provide the truest and therefore best art. At the same time, however, Howells juxtaposes with these passages others that cast doubt on their validity. Just prior to this manifesto of the ordinary, the narrator describes his own not Basil's observations of the Mohawk Valley and its Dutch farms, "a landscape that I greatly love for its mild beauty and tranquil picturesqueness." His vision of the land is a fictive combination of Washington Irving and his own fantasies, a pleasant vision that he knows "is not true" but has a value of its own. Basil and Isabel cannot have the same vision: she is ignorant, "as a true American woman," of history; he can call only on terrifying boyhood dreams of frontier massacres. "They cast an absurd [European] poetry over the whole landscape" and then turn away to the ordinary people on the train for their amusement.

The scene is intended as a metaphor for a transition in fiction, and implies that direct observation unblurred by conventions of romance leads one to truth and significance. Other scenes, however, suggest not only that that is false but that observations may gain their very significance from the needs and biases of observers and from such conventions. The most startling example of distorted observation, of course, is the silk-hatted gentleman on the night boat. The boat has run over "a common tow-boat" and badly injured its crew, as a witness reports. The smug, self-righteous silk-cap twists the account to coincide with his own—that "the tow-boat hit us"—and then displaces concern for any victims with a tale of his own "fearful escape" in another accident.

Going down the St. Lawrence later, Basil and Isabel observe a tall handsome man, who because of conventional images (dress, cross, ring, opera glass) they assume a European, "a hero" (117). He turns out to be—like the actually more refined Kitty Ellison—from western New York; and the Marches feel foolish. In waiting rooms and at meals throughout the journey (9, 113, 134), they observe people and infer more about them from gestures and behavior, as often as not erroneously. Like the poor German-American on the train, they misread the signs. The tastefully dressed Canadian girl from Kingston (112) can be interpreted as wealthy (Basil) or poor (Isabel) and leaves her observers with more questions than answers, and fictions based as much on observers' temperament as on anything she does.

Even Basil's own journal from an earlier trip—a factual document—is as remarkable now for its sentiment as its "touches of nature and reality," perhaps inseparable from the sentiment, for life in his youth was "a thing to be put into pretty periods" (159). Now, he laments, it is a business "that has risks and averages, and may be insured." So, he implies, is literature, whose very forms that incorporate "representative" observations are governed by a market patronage and in effect determine the truth-quality of their parts as much as the observed experiences do. Observations of the ordinary, therefore, do not themselves have significance, as the narrator says, but take on significance with the form that the observing—and the mediating—and the reading consciousnesses provide them.

The problem is established in terms of history. The beauty of Niagara is set against its violence, the violence of its history against the romantic histories of Francis Parkman, who made America's "meagre past wear something of the rich romance of old European days," who turned America's origins into "medieval chivalry," thereby identifying it with Europe's origins and actually illuminating it more than the "feeble glimmer of the guide-books" (89). Isabel and Basil turn all the primitive energies of that world into "entertaining fables" to incorporate Niagara into their wedding journey. Neither the natural fact nor the historical fact has clear significance without such incorporation, without being incorporated into the "journey" that early in the book is associated with life itself (20). Similarly, Basil paints for Isabel the stories of Cartier, Champlain, and Maisonneuve "using the colors of the historian who has made these scenes the beautiful inheritance of all dreamers" (139); and at Quebec they attend to the "romantic splendor and pathos" in the story of Montcalm and Wolfe. The significance of history, the book implies, lies in its imaginative and exemplary re-creation, for the totality of what happened lies inaccessible to the present (149).

As the significance of places Basil and Isabel visit is tied to signifying histories, so their own experiences are described as theatrical or dramatic. At times they are an audience for a scene acted out before them; at times they are actors. Once Howells even sets up lines of dialogue to make the point (41-42). At times they are playwrights fantasizing a drama out of what they observe. From the beginning, nature—the storm—itself is a theatrical pantomime (5). A scene between Kitty and Fanny Ellison is a "comedy" on which the Marches eavesdrop. The narrator calls them "both actors and spectators" in an "immense complex drama" which has "its *denouement* only in eternity" (44), now a mystery, now a farce, now a tragedy disguised as comedy.

Both the ship of fools and the stage of life are, of course, conventional images; but Howells adds that "each group had its travesty in some other; the talk of one seemed the rude burlesque, the bitter satire of the next," that mimesis is parodic, that the tone at least of the representation is not that of the original, that opposites moreover blur into one. The sorrowful widow in black and joyful bride in white blur into one in symbolizing mortality. The narrator self-consciously catches himself waxing romantic and in relief gives up the "stale effect" and "hackneyed characters" as night "drops her curtain" on the scene. But in the very next scene the boat is "topsy-turvy" during the tug-boat accident. To suggest the loss of surface order and control, Howells uses imagery of mistiness and disarray that establishes a mood of dreamy romance. Only the widow in black and the bride in white remain signs of the incident's reality. The boundary between fact and romance again becomes hazy. On their journey, Basil and Isabel see several parodies, travesties of their own situation, couples or individuals comparable to themselves, as the narrator from the beginning says they will (7). Those persons, of course, are also originals and have secondary or parodic significance only in relation to an observation from the Marches' position. If they, like the Marches, moreover, keep trying to appear what they are not, even that signification is dubious.[4]

At the end, Howells returns to the theatrical motif. A troupe of actors, giving *Pygmalion* in Montreal, stay at the same Quebec hotel as the Marches. Basil sees them, therefore, off stage, yet finds in them the charm of Spanish romance, finds their reality more theatrical than the stage. The "commonness and cheapness of the *mise en scène* ... give it an air of fact and make it like an episode of fiction" (172). The actors seem "to be playing rather than living the life of strolling players." Though picturesque, the scene seems to be validating a fiction close to fact or reality;

but actually it articulates a reality that does not distinguish itself from theatre, history, or romance. Basil himself and the narrator turn the actors into their own picturesque, a fiction closer to misinterpretations and fanciful interpretations than to an empirically ascertained reality.

The stage remained attractive for Howells not only for its lure of money and fame, but also because as he developed his representational aesthetic it provided a medium in which living persons could enact representative experiences without the distortions of a purely verbal medium. A few years later Turgenev's novels profoundly influenced Howells in part because he was already predisposed toward dramatic techniques and found in Turgenev the best model for the use of such techniques in fiction. The actors in *Their Wedding Journey*, however, are part of a reality not clearly distinguished from theatre, history, or romance and perhaps not accessible except through the conventions of those forms. Art forms—such as plays and notions about plays and actors—govern Basil's very perception of the actors as much as empirical observation or perception delimits any art based on such observations. *Their Wedding Journey*, like other novels that set out to reduce the gap between verbal art and reality, continually reveals its own artifice and the artifice of Realism.

The troupe performs *Pygmalion*, a play about the difference between nature and culture, one in which art sets the norm for life. Howells continued to enact the Pygmalion story in his own career. By validating a new set of myths for modern America, that practically effaced the recent disastrously traumatic war and that ameliorated the harshest consequences of finance capitalism, Howells could influence the course of America and also validate the role of the writer. As originator of the new man and woman, he could have both Godlike and Adamic qualities, helping to create that new world while being the namer of the creatures he found there.

After the Civil War had justified Hawthorne's, not Emerson's, hypothesis of a new American Eden, Americans needed new models of origin different from Bancroft's romantic myth of American destiny. Local color manifested one sentiment, medievalism another, but business progressivism fostered a third that was more adaptable to the times. It nurtured a myth of individualism, a "Bildungs" pattern in which the life and growth of the child become adult could be a constantly renewable model. The middle-class basically accepted a dehistoricized version of that model. Howells was its American authorizer, but without the "Bildungs," without informing childhoods. His protagonists rarely have significant pasts prior to the action of the novel. Like Thoreau they are starting out anew in the morning of the book. The model, moreover, is generally masculine. Women, even when more attractive than male characters, are also more static.

The most excruciating "fable of disaster" Basil and Isabel have experienced is not the Civil War but their own "broken engagement," at best a pallid metaphor for the national tragedy. Like America they are surrounded by commerce, and their experience makes "their present fortune more prosperous." Meanwhile on the city streets one morning, they become "the first man and first woman in the garden of the new-made earth" and set out to rename the animals, albeit with "the most graceful euphemisms" (23). In that great age of euphemism, Howells could re-signify the war as a "broken engagement." Basil might be speaking of Howells' book as well as his own trip when he says that "as this was their first journey together in America, he wished to give it at the beginning as pungent a national character as possible, and ... could imagine nothing more peculiarly American than a voyage to New York by a Fall River boat" (5).

Their journey, despite Howells' Realism, is an active metaphor—a re-naming of America as they move simultaneously into past and future, origins and frontiers. It opens in the oppressive heat and bustling commerce of New York, "the weariness of selling" and "the weariness of buying," the sterility of the Battery. They fantasize "eternal demolition and construction of the city," ridding it of "odious" fellow-passengers and repopulating it with proper vacationers. No Whitmanesque working-class vision, their fiction is one in which urban workers—hotel clerks, ticket agents, cabmen—are denigrated, and interest is located in vacationers like the Ellisons. At first Boston seems to be a positive image, set in thematic opposition to New York; but to Basil the outsider, Isabel's home town is snobbish and elitist even if it does patronize artists (19, 24, 64, 159, 167), and finally Boston is left outside the book's dialectic. So, curiously enough, is small-town America, Howells' own roots and *the* image of America for many in the United States. He had intended a chapter on Jefferson, Ohio, but left it out—perhaps because he feared "giving offense" to family friends, perhaps because it no longer seemed essential to the book, perhaps because it awkwardly complicated his themes.[5] Instead there is a romantic chapter on Rochester, an "enchanting" site on the boundary between commerce and nature, between flour mills and the Genessee Falls. Basil himself can there authorize, moreover, a changed version of the Sam Patch legend in which the particular, "'Springt der Sam Patsch kuhn und frei,'" is translated into the general, "'Leaps a figure bold and free'" (70).

From Rochester the Marches travel west to Niagara, their closest stopping place to the frontier, the spot where they meet the "refined" Westerner, Kitty Ellison. Howells' picture of Niagara is less captivating than that by Henry Adams in *Esther*, but its association with primitive natural force is emphasized. So is, however, its confinement, its control by tourism and hydraulic canals (97). It is natural power controlled, an appropriate symbol for entrepreneurial America. The Indians have been distorted into silk-hatted Protestants and girls named Daisy Smith. If they cannot be suitable primitives, such creatures "ought to be fading away," or so Isabel says.[6]

Niagara, affiliated with weddings and honeymoons, suggests not only natural force controlled but sexuality controlled, for marriage is social control of sex. Marriage, in fact, became the central problem in Howells' fiction from then on, as it not only continued a convention in nineteenth-century fiction but also provided a means for working out conflicts related to power and authority in a once "edenic" country.[7] Howells'own supposedly prudish personality is often tied to his treatment of femininity, but his repeated attention here to marriage suggests an even more deliberate pattern. The trip on which the novel was based was, of course, not a honeymoon for Howells and Elinor, but took place several years after their European wedding (alluded to by means of references to the European courtship of Basil and Isabel). Some of the particulars were drawn from a follow-up trip Howells took with his father. The book, however, is full of imagery and discussions of brides, marriages, hiding bridal appearances, alternatives to marriage (such as convents), and of course the mighty Niagara.

> Here within the compass of a mile, those inland seas of the North, Superior, Huron, Michigan, Erie, and the multitude of smaller lakes, all pour their floods, where they swirl in dreadful vortices, with resistless under-currents boiling beneath the surface of that mighty eddy. Abruptly from this scene of secret power, so different from the thunderous splendors of the cataract itself, rise lofty cliffs on every side, to a height of two hundred feet, clothed from the water's edge almost to their crests with dark cedars. Noiselessly, so far as your senses perceive, the lakes steal out of the whirlpool, then, drunk and wild, with brawling rapids roar away to Ontario through the narrow channel of the river. (101)

Yet this maelstrom formed by the immense inland seas of America, this center of both natural calamities and a history of war, is, Howells humorously contends, no match for newlyweds:

> They are of all manners of beauty, fair and dark, slender and plump, tall and short; but they are all beautiful with the radiance of loving and being loved. Now, if ever in their lives, they are charmingly dressed, and ravishing toilets take the willing eye from the objects of interest. How high the heels of the pretty boots, how small the tender-tinted gloves, how electrical the flutter of the snowy skirts! What is Niagara to these things? (84-85)

The place is, in fact, almost abandoned to bridal couples, and any
one out of his honeymoon is in some degree an alien there, and
must discern a certain immodesty in his intrusion. Is it for his pro-
fane eyes to look upon all that blushing and trembling joy? A man
of any sensibility must desire to veil his face, and, bowing his
excuses to the collective rapture, take the first train for the wicked
outside world to which he belongs. (84)

The language of prurience dominates. He who is not part of the marriage
game contributes to wickedness. Niagara is the place to affirm control
over the sexual and the female, as Basil does at Three Sisters Island.
There Isabel cowers in feminine fear of recrossing the bridge, and finally
crosses only because of a threat to her vanity. Raw Niagara threatens the
marriage bond, as Isabel implies when, entranced by its strange dreadful
force, she whimsically and theatrically warns Basil, "'I'm no longer
yours, Basil; I'm most unhappily married to Niagara. Fly with me, save
me from my awful lord!'" (103).[8]

Howells' most explicit connection between his sexual and national
themes lies in an adjacent passage in which he associates "public love-
making" with "pleasure-travel" and "every famous American landscape."
In the village and the wilds, "new-wedded lovers with their interlacing
arms and their fond attitudes" represent America as a new "Arcady," a
new "golden age" (90). Howells' tenuous connection between this theme
and the recent war is more clumsily handled, by means of a "sad-faced
patrician" of "half-barbaric, homicidal gentility of manner," a Southerner
whose appearance calls forth from abolitionist Basil an attack on post-war
sentimentalization of plantations" but also a corresponding compassion
for the "impoverished" former slaveholder, "the beaten rebel" (97).

As the Marches reverse directions and stop moving towards the frontier, toward natural origins, they in effect turn back towards Europe, as it
is most clearly present in America, that is in French Canada. As they tour
churches with the smug superiority of progressive Protestants slumming
in the romance of primitive superstition, Howells develops a critical perspective on the gap between Europe and America. Canada has a
continuity with its European past (124), he says, that his own country
lacks. It is a bonding that may be an advantage but may also invite
sentimentality: to venerate outdated forms, to build monuments to Nelson
not to "the local past and its heroic figures" (140), to control sexuality and
"the most precious part of ... woman's nature" (127-28) in the "narrow
cells" of convents not in marriage. Howells, however, turns the criticism
back on his own country, whose travelers are also far too willing to find
"precious" the "ruins and impostures and miseries and superstitions" of
Europe (125). He wrote this at a time when genealogy services, marriage
to titled families, and diverse cultural imitations were coming into vogue

and, like the copyright crisis with which he draws an explicit comparison (134), were surely endangering Howells' hopes for and myth of the American writer.

Economic conditions, moreover, he implies, determine cultural dependency. Canada remains an "unmanly boy, clinging to the maternal skirts" because goods thereby remain cheaper than in the more independent United States. On the other hand, although Canada cannot pull loose from English apron strings, the United States has turned over control to "the shabby despots who govern New York, and the swindling railroad kings whose word is law to the whole land" (135). The narrator criticizes "America" for its surrender to commercial values and "the almighty dollar" (43, 60, 135-36), but curiously attributes that materialistic sin mostly to the American female. It is Isabel who by means of a shilling buys herself off from a guilty feeling in a French cathedral (157). It is Isabel, that new-world Eve, who smuggles goods out of Canada and tempts Basil to adjust his own conscience. It is for Isabel that Basil forsakes his Muse to be an insurance salesman, as if the "feminization of American culture" has driven out true poetry.

Along with its cautious optimism, the book asserts a kind of masculine authority. From the beginning the narrator patronizingly would allow a woman to be "of Isabel's age, if she is of good heart and temper" (4). Women, however, if uncourted endure a "sad patience" (8). Isabel, "like all daughters of a free country," knows nothing about politics and economics (19), despite the threat of female suffrage (13), and, "as a true American woman," is woefully ignorant of history (54, 66). Women are vulnerable to fashion, vanity, and aristocracy (56, 93, 116). Such comments dot the entire narrative, and give shape to a fiction of masculine control, one which implies a concern with authority over subject matter, national audience, and the literary profession.

On their return to Boston, the Marches not only find the expected "drouth and heat, which they had briefly escaped," but also experience some discontent (178). Basil walks toward work and finds no camaraderie. To an acquaintance he seems to need a vacation, not to be returning from one. The workaday world has reasserted itself. Fiction, like their journey, is a green-world respite from work, but as the concluding dialogue implies, can be, unlike the sentimental domestic romances of the day, of significant relevance to American readers.

Notes

1. The letters and comments most directly relevant to the composition of *Their Wedding Journey* are quoted in the Introduction by John K. Reeves to his edition of the book (Bloomington: Indiana UP, 1968). References to the novel are to this edition. Also useful are the two biogra-

phies—Edwin H. Cady, *The Road to Realism* (Syracuse: Syracuse UP, 1956), and Kenneth S. Lynn, *William Dean Howells: An American Life* (New York: Harcourt Brace Jovanovich, 1971).

2. See John K. Reeves, "The Limited Realism of Howells' *Their Wedding Journey*," *PMLA* 77 (1962): 617-28; William M. Gibson, "Materials and Form in Howells' First Novels," *American Literature* 19 (1947): 158-66; and David L. Frazier, "*Their Wedding Journey*: Howell's Fictional Craft," *New England Quarterly* 42 (1969): 323-49.

3. Kenneth Seib deals with the book as an allegory of the "quest for the American character." See "Uneasiness at Niagara: Howells' *Their Wedding Journey*," *Studies in American Fiction* 4 (1976): 15-25. Henry Nash Smith makes several insightful comments on Howells' search for a fictional method in "Fiction and the American Ideology: The Genesis of Howells' Early Realism," in *The American Self: Myth, Ideology, and Popular Culture*, ed. S. B. Girgus (Albuquerque: U of New Mexico P, 1981) 43-57.

4. On this scene also see Marion W. Cumpiano, "The Dark Side of *Their Wedding Journey*," *American Literature* 40 (1969): 472-86.

5. W. D. Howells, *Selected Letters*, ed. G. Arms *et al.* (Boston: Twayne, 1979) 1:361.

6. Howells, like Twain, had little use for popular images of Indians as Noble Savages. He praised Francis Parkman for helping us to "desentimentalize" the loss of "uninteresting races." See *Atlantic Monthly* 25 (1870): 122-24.

7. See Allen F. Stein, "Marriage in Howells's Novels," *American Literature* 48 (1977): 501-24. The article is included, in a slightly different form, in *After the Vows Were Spoken: Marriage in American Literary Realism* (Columbus: Ohio State UP, 1984).

8. Gary A. Hunt, in the first article to explore fully the sexual patterns in this novel, emphasizes the Niagara scene (Isabel's "discovery of her own sexuality") and the Quebec scene (Basil's "sense of sexual loss"). To Hunt the novel shows Howells' ability "to project the suppressed underside of the Victorian mind." See "'A Reality That Can't Be Quite Definitely Spoken': Sexuality in *Their Wedding Journey*," *Studies in the Novel* 9 (1977): 17-32. For a discussion of related themes see Elizabeth Stevens Prioleau, *The Circle of Eros: Sexuality in the Work of William Dean Howells* (Durham, NC: Duke UP, 1983). One interesting early passage in the novel (10) connects the broken engagement with Basil's voracious appetite. A wife with "her slender relishes" and "dainty habits of lunching" cannot adjust to her husband's capacity for "eating at all hours of the day and night—as they write it on the sign-boards of barbaric eating-houses."

4

A Chance Acquaintance:
How Fiction Would Mean

A Chance Acquaintance, entitled "Romance of a Summer" in one working draft, is generally considered Howells' first true novel. Tracing relationships among several tourists in Quebec, it retained traits of the travel book, but also firmed up Howells' reputation as a writer of fiction. While he was establishing editorial control over the *Atlantic Monthly*, it provided him a means for working through ambivalent feelings about Boston. In effect it became a way to define what such things as "Boston" and "the West" would mean in post-war America, and therefore it also forced Howells to face seriously the problems of signification and meaning in fiction.

Sales of *A Chance Acquaintance* in 1873 were modest, but reviews good, and a number of friends and fellow writers praised the book.[1] Not long after publication Howells wrote his father that it was important because "it sets me forever outside of the rank of mere *culturists*, followers of an elegant literature, and proves that I have sympathy with the true spirit of Democracy."[2] At that time he was taking an advanced position in supporting farmers' unions against powerful railroads, and felt that in both form and theme *A Chance Acquaintance* aligned him with liberalism against imitative and invidious forces in the East.

Howells realized that there were limitations to the kind of fiction he had written in *Their Wedding Journey*. Because it allowed little development of dramatic characterization, it tended toward a repetitious abstraction. He wrote James Comly that he could not "write two W. Js."[3] The opening of *A Chance Acquaintance*, however, still connects places such as Boston or the West with meanings and values. Boston at first signifies the Marches in their genteel charm. Kitty has "sworn a sisterhood" with Isabel, and writes Uncle Jack that he has "not rated Boston people a bit too high." It also signifies the noble antislavery cause that has been Dr. Ellison's lifelong commitment. After emancipation, in fact, "the doctor did live for an ideal Boston" (7). The rest of his energies went into a search for significant origins: he studied the Mound Builders, the origin of the United States in Faneuil Hall, points of "ancient colonial interest," and the origins of abolitionism.

"The West" is tied not to abstract ideas of reformism but to the bloody actuality of Kansas violence. It is a place where people like Kitty's own father learn to oppose slavery not from general teachings but from actual interaction with border ruffians. It is also symbolized by the burned-over districts of western New York, site of both evangelical and antislavery fervor, a place where idealistic but humorless abolitionist speakers like everyone else can be the butt of frontier humor and where genteel conventions do not yet govern. It is the locus of a more practical democracy (37) than that of Boston itself, even though that city signifies an ideal and an origin.

Early in the story the two characters who come to stand in different ways for their respective regions are Kitty Ellison for the West and Miles Arbuton for Boston. Their descriptions are repeatedly linked to their areas. Howells, moreover, sets the novel not in the actual West nor in New England but at a neutral site—Quebec—that is New World with new world scenery and rusticity but also Old World with the French language, a cathedral, Catholic churches, and historical associations (including some with America's Revolution). Characters have regionally differentiated traits. The setting for their drama consists of aspects associated with each character's region, yet is itself distinctive. Howells thereby sets up his fiction with thematic counters like those in earlier romances, that is, without the distancing haze of Hawthorne's fables, the exaggerated incidents of Cooper's adventures and the explicit dialectics of Melville's allegories.[4]

Kitty and Arbuton are not tokens in an allegory but "types" in a more or less representational narrative. To Henry James, Kitty was charming because she suggested a "type" and the tale foreshadowed "a conflict between her type and another." He also suggested that the ending was weakened because Howells had made Arbuton behave too shabbily, but he was unsure whether the failure was one of mishandling the particular courtship or misinterpreting the type.[5] In some ways Howells, who always loved the theatre and more than once tried to succeed as a dramatist, shifted in *A Chance Acquaintance* from the mode of the travel book to dramatic conventions. His characters signify at times like those in the old comedy of humors but move around like those in an eighteenth-century comedy of manners by Sheridan or Goldoni. Side trips around Quebec are generated to provide a setting for liaisons between Kitty and Arbuton. As they carry on their courtship, Howells develops other themes around them, such as regional differentiation.

Arbuton does not signify all of Boston, for in "representative" typology characters do not signify all of such conglomerates as cities or nations; and, moreover, Howells has explicitly set other "Boston" signs in opposition to Arbuton—for example the Marches and those antislavery leaders and writers who established Boston's intellectual and cultural preeminence. Arbuton, therefore, is not "Boston" but a type of Bostonian with traits, of course, not limited to Bostonians.[6] Drawn from both observation and literary models (Kitty remarks she has seen such as Arbuton in novels but not in life), he is a composite of traits that both repulse and seduce Howells—and Kitty. The critical consensus is that Arbuton is an insufferable snob, whom the pert and sassy Kitty cannot continue to tolerate. Howells, to be sure, tried hard to make *A Chance Acquaintance* add up to that, but it does not. Arbuton has positive traits and is a more magnetic image in the text than is Kitty despite the tendency to sentimentalize her.

Even the ending, in which Arbuton comes off very "shabby," is problematic. Howells' own career depended on leaving places like provincial Eriecreek for Boston. Therefore, returning to Eriecreek while Arbuton returns to Boston is hardly a triumph for Kitty. Moreover, Dick Ellison, who generally articulates common sense, if a boorish common sense (after all, he enjoys Twain, Shakespeare, and Cervantes, but disdains popular romances), speculates that Kitty really ran away from a difficult scene and felt inadequate to what lay ahead for her in Boston. The surface of the text marks him as literally wrong, but the suggestion is psychologically valid. Empirical observation, after all, has been both undermined and validated in the book. Only the writer can authoritatively draw significance from observation, and only the reader meaning from that significance.

Arbuton and Kitty were both very personal figures for Howells, and cross-sexual patterns of authorial identification led to curious inconsistencies in characterization. An apparent guilt over his own identification with Arbuton severely restricted the freedom of development Howells allowed that character. Arbuton's repressions are given as the cause for his tight behavior; but Howells' own may be a cause for the tightness in his characterization. A corresponding sentimentalization of Kitty's traits resulted in some uncertainty because Howells combined her dreamy romanticism with her pert candor.

Early in the text Ellison uses the nickname "Boston" to denote Arbuton, and the city is frequently mentioned in connection with his behavior. The initial misperception of him as an Englishman—recalling a similar misperception of a *western New Yorker* for a foreign dignitary in *Their Wedding Journey*—makes a point about cultural imitation and dependency in America that is later validated. At the same time that Arbuton is defined against Kitty, he is also defined against both the friendly charm of the Marches and the "New Jerusalem" of intellectual and political leadership. As Boston can mean (for Howells, Kitty, and America) the open bourgeois gentility of Basil and Isabel, so too can it mean the ideals of our "magnanimous democracy" in which one is valued for what he is, not for his color, wealth, or family (8). But Boston can, as Howells through Arbuton asserts, also mean imitativeness, snobbery, and repression. Despite a genuine interest in them, Miles disdains people "he might have to drop for reasons of society." He has the habit of "protecting himself from the chances of life" (11). He shuns the Ellisons' coarse drollery, condescendingly wishes to avoid spoiling their voyage, patronizes native scenery that lacks historical significance (17), and is repeatedly described as cold (42, 50, 89). Even so the ending is forced. Arbuton may be a cold snob, but he is impeccably well mannered, and in a real world he would probably not ignore Kitty completely in the final scene, as Howells makes him do in order to carry out his planned ending.

Arbuton is also sincere and just, a man of purity and rectitude (39), one who would have become a Protestant minister had he been neither so liberal in his creed nor so squeamish toward poverty. He is a man of intelligence, politeness, and taste. He bravely protects Kitty from a vicious dog; he is charitable; and he is physically strong enough to hurl a rock further than anyone else on board the boat. Despite the gloves and thin umbrella that go with him—as pipe and scarf go with Ellison—and possibly mark him as effete, Arbuton has a magnetic masculinity that is different from the coarser midwestern masculinity of Ellison. With a name that perhaps alludes to Miles Coverdale and his failed romance, but is explicitly connected to Miles Standish and his colonial lineage as well as to Standish's own failed romance, Arbuton loses his case—but not to a younger John Alden.

The Priscilla of this story, however, is very much attracted to Miles. Although she is linked with the West (42) and the spirit of democracy (37), she is content with neither. Eriecreek is for her no garden or attractive frontier set against a corrupt city. It is an ugly town, peopled by "mortally dull, narrow, and uncongenial" residents. Kitty, like many an American (including Howells), aspires to "see more of the world that she had found so fair … London, Venice, Rome, those infinitely older and more storied cities of which she had lately talked so much with Mr. Arbuton" (145). She even considers marrying him "for the sake of a bridal trip to Europe," and in self-deprecation is "anxious to be tested" by the light of Boston (145). As Dick Ellison jests, "wherever Americans go, they like to be presented at court" (149).

The cradle of American independence, Boston has become not only a goal in itself but the gateway to European re-attachment. Kitty in her romantic dreaminess imagines herself "meant for an old country," at least one "with dormer-windows," to which Fanny replies, "'Well then, Kitty, I don't see what you're to do but to marry East and live East; or else find a rich husband, and get him to take you to Europe to live'" (57).[7]

Kitty is not offended by Arbuton's invidious distinctions, but rather is "inspired" by his "Boston of mysterious prejudices and lofty reservations ... that found its social ideal in the Old World" (91). The consequence is insecurity and doubt in her own self, even "a languid self-contempt" (92). So for all of Kitty's "natural simplicity" and pert, independent, democratic Westernness, she is predominantly characterized by dreamy, romantic literariness and an attraction to Old World manners. Fanny says her love for literature is reason to "live in a place where everybody is literary and intellectual" (128); but her literary predispositions are as mixed as Howells' own. A happy, dreamy romantic from her first appearance (3), she is known to have once penned some "childish" fictions of her own. Now she peoples stock romances with the quaint *habitans* she observes or imagines picturesque narratives around their appearances (76, 89). Although her dreamy romanticism is linked to her femininity, she also articulates a notion of fiction related to Howells' own emerging Realism.

At one point Kitty and Miles discuss a new book named *Details*, which Kitty praises for being "just the history of a week in the life of some young people who happen together in an old New-England country-house; nothing extraordinary, little, every-day things told so exquisitely, and all fading naturally away without any particular result, only the full meaning of everything brought out." What "the full meaning of everything" is, or rather what such a phrase refers to, is not clear, though it would seem that Howells himself aspires to some related mode of signification. There is but "the slightest sort of plot," so one mode of romantic signification is minimized; to Arbuton's chagrin, all fades "naturally away without any particular result" (98). Full meaning does not seem to imply an allegorical process, but Kitty would take pleasure in finding out the beauties of "poverty-stricken subjects," perhaps by a correspondence between physical and spiritual truths such as that assumed by Emerson a generation earlier. Kitty's comments imply an epiphanic mode of significance, and, like James, Howells learned from the Romantic poets how to incorporate that mode into his fiction and how to use it to assert fictive authority, though very little Howells criticism mentions it.

Arbuton suspects the author of *Details* (which a number of readers erroneously inferred to be an actual novel) "found too much meaning in everything," a skeptical position he further defines as a masculine position, for women are capable of seeing "more than we do in a little space" (98). The dilemma is at the center of Howellsian Realism, especially in so far as the causal pattern in a "plot" is minimized so as not to carry a major message, and such elements as character and setting are foregrounded. To what extent do particulars carry general significance? The word "character" itself has at times even meant a mark or symbol in writing, and comes from the Latin for an instrument to make marks. Although it can describe aspects of real persons—"He is of good character" or "He is a real character"—as a word meaning "person" it has largely been limited to fictional constructs and suggests as well "standing for something" thematically—that is, not standing for something allegorically but signifying to readers or audience some category or type of thematic significance.

In literature governed by Neoplatonic models or by Idealism, the signification by which a narrative character could stand for a Reality (such as Good Deeds or Faith) was understood by writer and audience. The new world of middle-class commerce was also a world of empiricism and, in effect, nominalism, albeit rarely called that. Although the seventeenth and eighteenth centuries continued to produce allegory, including John Bunyan's, less often it was allegory in which the "tenors" were abstractions and more often allegory in which tenors were particular persons, places, or events.

As the comedy of humors gave way to the comedy of manners, and as the novel developed in middle-class culture, signification of abstract realities gave way to signification of characterological types, and they themselves signified in two ways: by a new set of stock and internally meaningful literary conventions and by external reference to a social world known by author and reader. If, as Barbara Hardy says, the novel is intrinsically self-reflexive, it is so not only because of the peculiar nature of narrative voice but also because the novel must somehow inscribe within itself its own mode of signification. Rarely is that mode allegorical; but rarely also does a character not function as a sign. Even those most formalist of critics who resist allegorizing of a text would find a character not signifying as extraneous to structure.

Howells sought a rationale for prose fiction like that Wordsworth set for poetry in his Preface to *Lyrical Ballads*. Making his way in an eastern literary establishment whose traditions were necessary even as they were replaced or overthrown, he sought an intellectually and socially significant fiction freed from its romance conventions. As a trained journalist he could draw well on observations from daily life; but unlike political journalism, even the most realistic fiction depends in limited ways on empirical observation. The rest is imaginative extension that defines a significance or message for the work. Using the particulars of ordinary experience, at times in a curiously apologetic way, Howells occasionally approaches a kind of social allegory like that in the fiction of Cooper.[8] The conflict between characters comes to stand for social thematics in rather paraphrasable ways. Apparent failures of composition—not allowing characters to work out destiny in ways consistent with their early presentation—are manifestations of Howells' control of thematic direction and, of course, a form of wish fulfillment. In effect, the explicit thematics of his novels are only part of their message. The rest is the validation, by sheer re-presentation, of an American middle class with a central role for the writer-observer and a fantasied effacement of the cruelest aspects of capitalist growth that actually brought that class into existence and that made possible a William Dean Howells, even as it determined his role.

None of Howells' Bostonian signs in these first books have much to do with commerce, except for Basil's reluctant turn from literature to the insurance business, a change, of course, not without autobiographical significance for the new editor of the *Atlantic*. The businessman is middle America's Dick Ellison of Milwaukee; but commerce, questions of production, sales, and finance, are far more significant by their absence from Howells' early books than by their presence. He himself was constantly engaged in a struggle to write enough, to bargain enough, and to understand a new kind of audience in order to keep up a respectable life-style. He valued the model of the self-made man; and in the America he was describing, that was becoming less and less separable from commerce. In Howells' eight early novels, however, money is at best a hidden issue, never foregrounded as cause or effect. Then, when it does become central, as in *A Modern Instance*, Howells also confronts a set of other serious problems and suffers a breakdown before he can complete the text.

Questions of power and control, however, are not absent from these works but are articulated through the courtship and marriage theme, at times with such correlative motifs as nature and religion. *A Chance Acquaintance* does not have the powerful central image of Niagara with its natural and sexual connotations, its associations with marital controls of sex; but it does establish "nature" as a sign for an uncontrolled and unrefined aspect of the world. Although some critics connect Kitty to a "natural" West against Arbuton's refined East, her cousin Fanny hates nature and is the most theatrical of characters. Her own simplicity, moreover, is due as much to her youth as to her region. It is Miles, not Howells, who may see her as something "natural," since she is actually a bookish town girl, not a rustic maid. Nature is not regional but continental. It is not western scenery but American scenery that Arbuton fails to appreciate because it lacks historic associations. Nature itself is neutral in *A Chance Acquaintance* it is desolate, bleak, and barren as often as it is beautiful (13, 41, 45). Its attraction comes with control—when it becomes "scenery," when it can be sublime or, more likely, "picturesque" (29, 87), and when it can be associated with a literary work like *Evangeline* or with history. Arbuton and Kitty are not so far apart in their method of enjoying nature, only in their education. The natural, however, is also what Arbuton has repressed. Once in a while, as Kitty says, Miles loses that total self-control, "his training doesn't hold out, and he seems to have nothing natural to fall back upon" (90). While hurling rocks against the cliffs of Cape Eternity, "he exulted in a sense of freedom ... as if for an instant he had rent away the ties of custom, thrown off the bonds of social allegiance, broken down and trampled upon the conventions which his whole life long he had held so dear and respectable" (46). He is then appalled at his own behavior, which might seem as vulgar as that of the uninhibited, garrulous "Canadian lady of ripe age," whom Arbuton disdains but whom Kitty sees as material for a "touching romance" (48). In catching himself, Miles realizes he came perilously close to "shaking hands with the shabby Englishman in the Glengarry cap, or ... asking the whole admiring company of passengers down to the bar" (46).

Howells designates Miles's temporary release as healthy behavior, but dangerous—"his broken defenses," his will to reassert "the spirit of his college days," to trample on repressive conventions. When Arbuton recovers, he lashes out, surprisingly, at Ellison, who represents for him "everything that was aggressively and intrusively vulgar" (47), but who, like Mark Twain, stands in Howells' eyes for a healthy mixture of manners and will. It is through his courtship of Kitty, in effect, that Miles seeks to reassert what is left of his will in a controlled form. Whatever mixture she signifies for Howells, for Miles she is a natural, sexual beauty.

Religious imagery functions in a way similar to nature. Miles Arbuton is a "divine possibility ... invested with a halo of romance" for Kitty (10). A "pretty domestic presence, a household priestess ordering the temporary Penates," she is so impressed by him that she feels through his lips "a god spoke" (55). He is for her to "revere" not respect: "'say *revere*, Fanny; say revere!'" (89). Her bliss in her engagement to him is "divine" (150). It is in the old Jesuit Residence at Sillery that a guide mistakes them for a married couple and, with a line that explicitly makes a connection with the earlier novel, says, "'I suppose this is your wedding journey'" (119). Moreover, at the oldest church in Quebec, where Kitty aesthetically empathizes with a poor suppliant, Arbuton's *caritas* stimulates Kitty's *eros*. The Ursuline Convent, adjacent to her hotel, stimulates her literary fancy, as she turns the nuns' lives into stories of tragic love, as she finds all of Quebec "crying out to be put into historical romances!" (78). Like nature, religious devotion represents massive energy requiring control. In Howells' next novel, *A Foregone Conclusion*, he uses the overlap between religious and sexual force to develop further a parallel between sexual and literary authority.

The reader's problem with such scenes is not one of knowing what happens but one of knowing what it signifies thematically. The characterization of Arbuton and Kitty seems clear enough but the extent to which Howells intends to make them stand for regional or sexual values may be less clear. In this early novel Howells was trying to develop an adequate mode of fictional signification. Like *Their Wedding Journey*, *A Chance Acquaintance* is composed in a flat but subtle style that tends to efface the authorial narrator. It reports ordinary events but on a trip that is rather special for the sojourners. It combines credible travel-book descriptions with representative dialogue in order to create surface verisimilitude in the natural but exotic world of Quebec. From the beginning, moreover, the novel authorizes reading in terms of a geographical dialectic. It also authorizes figurative interpretations of Nature and Religion and connects them with issues of sexuality and possession. Characters and objects are not only representative types but also tend toward a social allegory. Commonplace incidents, such as rock-throwing, are laden with figurative significance.

The entire courtship, in fact, is framed by two such innocent incidents, Kitty's unintentional grasp of Arbuton's arm and Arbuton's neglect of Kitty at Lorette. A psychoanalytical model is hardly necessary to translate both episodes into wish fulfillment or fantasy, since Howells so fully contextualizes them with authorial suggestions. The extent of their allegorical implications is more problematic. The passengers on the Saguenay boat have been amusedly witnessing an Indian wedding party at Cacouna, an incident used to indicate comically both the courtship motif and the nature/culture dichotomy operating in the romance. Like the opening descriptions of Kitty and Miles and the valorization of Boston and the West, the episode not only develops a theme but sets up rules or codes for subsequent thematic development. In any case, Kitty reaches out, it would seem, to take the arm of her masculine military kinsman and, he having stepped aside, unwittingly takes Arbuton's arm instead. The fact is clear enough—"what he was to do was not so plain" (15). Nor is what the reader is to do so plain until one reflects that the opening chapters catalog Kitty's desire to go East, to Boston or Europe, to go toward everything Arbuton might represent. Although in one framework the critical issue is an analysis of Kitty's motives, in the other the issue is Howells' problem of signification: to what extent can *ordinary* lives, settings, episodes, and gestures signify convincingly? Howells said that no mere reflection of an everyday world was adequate to serious writing; but if the elements of a genteel world to which he had attached himself might signify meanings, he would, he felt, create a new sort of fiction.

When Kitty realizes her error, her response is "mingled horror and amusement," a signal to the reader of her ambivalence, the ambivalence that will characterize her desire to be wooed by "Boston" and her repulsion at what she desires. That same ambivalence will lead to a "blissful" engagement from which she will paradoxically seek to extricate herself.

This gesture and, one might add, Arbuton's own ambivalent response symbolize the area that the narrative drama will explore; and, in fact, errors in critical interpretation of such texts generally result not from reading "figuratively" but from reducing the figurative play in the text to a simplistic pattern. Henry James, in a sense, has proved more amenable to modern criticism partly because he more openly chose a psychological space for his subject matter and thereby more explicitly insisted on figurative interpretation of resonant central images. Howells' own windy aesthetics of Realism have encouraged the simplest adoption of reflection theory in his criticism and have restricted understanding of both the intentional figurative dimensions of his books and his participation in a developing middle-class hegemony.

This crucial gesture not only signifies an emotional complex in the characters but calls attention to itself as a gesture or sign. What, the text asks, should a reader make of such an image in this text? What should an observer-writer make of such an image when he observes it, and when he replicates it in fiction? What should a participant make of it? This was a crucial period when "social science" was differentiated into economics, political science, sociology, and so forth, and when particular social sciences were seeking both a language and an epistemology, a model by which the relationship between observed particulars, system, and significances might be conveyed with authority. Consequently, Howells simultaneously explored relationships between observable particulars, a system of types, and significance, and developed a rhetoric that might convey such relationships with authority. Empiricism in both cases was merely a tool, not an end.

The arm-taking episode helps to set up a field of play on which a series of social and psychological themes are engaged. These themes culminate at Lorette, where Arbuton promenades with two Bostonians and neglects his fiancée. This scene, too, becomes a resonant image. It is generally read as the epitome of Arbuton's snobbery and the assertion of Miss Kitty's western democratic pride. As such, it also articulates Howells' own contempt for the kind of pseudoaristocratic exclusiveness, the invidious snobbery that perplexed him in Boston and left Elinor and him outsiders even when he was most influential. At the same time, however, Howells undermines the clarity of this meaning by juxtaposing Ellison's uncharitable but creditable interpretation of Kitty's behavior with Kitty's own peremptory dismissal of Arbuton. Arbuton's walk with the haughty ladies begins with only a mechanical compliance on his part. Kitty is put off by their appearance but still longs for what they represent and fancies "that she could easily be friends with such a girl as that, if they met fairly" (156). She feels inadequate, however. It is she, not Arbuton, who imagines herself as a milkmaid, and she who has decided to wear countrified clothes. She who would do anything to get out of ugly Eriecreek is also reluctant to surrender herself to Boston—either to the masculine control of Arbuton, who "tramples" on her very self in his possession of her, or to the stripping away of her only cultural identity that would come with marriage. Miles passionately seeks to drive everything "Eriecreek" out of her personality, to remold her under the best light in Boston. She herself, so anxious to be tested by the "light of Boston," desiring that there he would repeat his love for her (a paradoxical confirmation), then dresses and behaves so as to make that approval most difficult when she is, figuratively at least, at "Boston."

Kitty's epiphany, her realization that Arbuton actually considers her unfit to be a Boston matron, is set in tension with Miles's own epiphany, a realization that "she had been the gentle person and he the vulgar one," that she had "suddenly grown beyond him" (160-61). Miles, in all his lust and snobbishness, has the integrity of his own self-knowledge and is "a man of scrupulous truth" (159). Kitty in all her charismatic innocence has less self-knowledge, has entertained the thought of using Miles for a European voyage, has played fast and loose with his affections. The myths and realities of a virgin West and a dominating yet refined East play themselves out vicariously through this courtship romance, as do Howells' own ambivalent personal feelings. He is the westerner desiring both the success and the status of the East, yet fearing the exploitation and redefiniton of himself by that world. He is also now the Bostonian not tempted at all to live full time in Eriecreek or Ohio, even delaying or canceling trips home during family difficulties.

By withholding her favors Kitty preserves her integrity in the face of both submission and patronizing neglect. Arbuton, however, has recognized his mistake and apologetically reasserts his love to Kitty; the reader thus becomes aware of his willingness to learn from his mistakes. Kitty, now superior by Arbuton's own admission, can turn him away with the threat of making life very hard for him if he persists. Nothing in her epiphany, however, has led her to believe that her romantic dreams of the East are themselves bad, and so the decision that assures her integrity of self at this moment also implicitly repudiates her fulfillment of self in time. At the very end she admits she might have been too cruel, thereby assuming Miles's continued desire for her, but rationalizes that what happened at Lorette was more important than his having saved her life. In effect the "life" that his offer has allowed her, the life she sought, is repudiated to maintain the protective shell of her other "life." At the end she, not Arbuton, is protected in a shell from her own natural impulses.

The very relativization of the meaning of Arbuton's neglect through his and Kitty's contrasted responses (and Ellison's and Fanny's) reinforces the novel's skeptical empiricism. As with the earlier arm-taking, the problem is pragmatic—not what happened, but now what to do. Arbuton's implicit but regretted rejection of Kitty and Kitty's explicit but contradictory rejection of Arbuton both correspond to fulfilled fantasies: in one case freedom from the desired but dangerous Other that is female because she is uncontrolled and unrefined; in the second case, freedom from the dominating and potentially destructive Other. At the same time, however, these reasons for rejection contradict the basic motivating fantasies of each character. Howells himself, one might say, can thumb his nose at Boston to preserve his own integrity, but has become "Boston" as he wished all along. He can also send the West a-packing but know that his desires are inseparable from his identity as a westerner. The actual differences between characters may not be as significant as the fantasies they have about each other. In the end, though, *A Chance Acquaintance* is not simply a domestic novel about a Boston snob getting his just desserts from a healthy American girl. It is an ambivalent romance in which Howells offers an apparent statement through fictional types while actually exploring a maze of contradictions beneath that statement, and in which he deploys a surface verisimilitude of the ordinary while actually exploring the meaning of meaning in representational fiction.

Notes

1. See the Introduction by Jonathan Thomas and David J. Nordloh to *A Chance Acquaintance* (Bloomington: Indiana UP, 1971). That text is also the source for all references in the article.

2. W. D. Howells, *Selected Letters*, ed. G. Arms and C. K. Lohmann (Boston: Twayne, 1979) 2:24.

3. W. D. Howells, *Selected Letters*, ed. G. Arms *et al.* (Boston: Twayne, 1979) 1:380.

4. For a discussion of these issues, and particularly Howells' semi-allegorical method in *Their Wedding Journey*, see Henry Nash Smith, "Fiction and the American Ideology: The Genesis of Howells' Early Realism," in *The American Self: Myth, Ideology, and Popular Culture*, ed. Sam B. Girgus (Albuquerque: U of New Mexico P, 1981) 43-57.

5. Howells, *Selected Letters* 2:41.

6. On Howells' ambivalence towards Boston, see Scott Alexander Dennis, "The Uninhabitable Place: The Rootlessness of W. D. Howells," Diss. Syracuse University, 1976. Kenneth S. Lynn also provides a sense of this ambivalence in *William Dean Howells: An American Life* (New York: Harcourt Brace Jovanovich, 1971).

7. On Howells' development of national and international themes, see Olov W. Fryckstedt, *In Quest of America: A Study of Howells' Early Development as a Novelist* (Cambridge: Harvard UP, 1958).

8. See the article on Cooper by Jane P. Tompkins, "No Apologies for the Iroquois: A New Way to Read the Leatherstocking Novels," *Criticism* 23 (1981): 24-41.

5

A Foregone Conclusion:
Howells' First Novel After Turgenev

Although Turgenev's novels had recently provided Howells with a new model for fiction, *A Foregone Conclusion* posed a problem for him, one that might be called the crisis of the ending. The romance form against which he saw himself writing had conventional denouements that he eschewed, as he generally resisted dominance of plot. In the romance, death was appropriate, if adjusted or sentimentalized to support enduring values of innocence and heroism. Courtships, unless undermined by imperfections of character, normally culminated in marriage. The English and continental novelists had established more latitude in the handling of social intercourse; but Howells' dilemma was that the audience for whom he wrote novels overlapped with the audience for whom he was becoming, in *Atlantic Monthly*, an arbiter of good literature. He could afford to go only so far in testing boundaries and conventions in one form if he were to maintain authority in the other.

Much is made of Howells' comment to Charles Eliot Norton that he would have preferred to end the story "with Don Ippolito's rejection." On the other hand, he once wrote H. H. Boyesen that the novel ended exactly as he had always planned.[1] In a sense both statements are sincere. The happy ending is bittersweet. Ferris never amounts to much as an artist, and lives on Florida's fortune. Ferris' relationship with Florida in Venice is not orchestrated to end in their permanent separation, which might render the irony of Don Ippolito's demise less poignant. As it is, the ultimate pathos of his "tragedy" is that to Ferris and Florida he becomes, finally, no more than "a mere problem" (171).[2] The almost melodramatic carelessness with which Howells tosses off the final chapter stands out in contrast to the minute care he brings to the rest of the novel. Henry James and others let him know their disappointment. It would be disingenuous to argue that the carelessness draws attention to itself as a parody of convention; yet the ending did serve Howells' purposes as much as the rest of the book did.

Each of Howells' novels in the 1870s after *Their Wedding Journey* developed a romance that might well end without fulfillment, but only in *A Chance Acquaintance* and *Private Theatricals* did he allow it to end so. In *A Foregone Conclusion* and *The Lady of the Aroostook* he tacked on marriages that satisfy conventions but leave problematic resolutions for major themes.[3] In all four cases weakness on the part of the male, coupled with either a character or situational defect in the female, has undermined a happy ending. In effect, attention is turned back away from plot to significations of character and place. Even in his two full-length plays of this period, which more or less had to end happily, Howells embedded problems that left the simple comic ending not so simple after all. In *Out of the Question*, although Blake can marry Leslie Bellingham, it is made quite clear that no normal self-made midwesterner can win the hand of a Brahmin lass. Only because, coincidentally, Blake in the Civil War rescued Leslie's own brother from drowning is he qualified to woo the sister. He is so, moreover, not on the brother's own endorsement, but on the mother's—in effect, by displacing the brother whose life he saved, by literally showing himself more of *the class* than the brother is. The play, however, is certainly not a general rebuttal to the implications of *A Chance Acquaintance*. In *A Counterfeit Presentiment* Bartlett can win the hand of fair Constance only, as it were, by a game of mirrors—by showing he is not the man the Wyatts think him to be, and then by showing Constance he is the man she did not know him to be and the other is not the man (indeed is a forger, a counterfeiter) she thought him to be.

After 1879, in a way, Howells took revenge on endings. In *The Undiscovered Country* and *Dr. Breen's Practice*, the marriages at the end are less important than other problems raised in the text, although they also are part of a troubled exploration of autonomy, control, responsibility, and sexual identity. In *A Modern Instance*, the culmination of Howells' early period, he did not end with the required romantic marriage but began with a marriage and let it disintegrate. After his own breakdown, *A Woman's Reason* and *Indian Summer* were attempts to recover order through strategic retreat. The crisis of ending in *A Foregone Conclusion* is not a simple struggle by Howells against romantic conventions, but a kind of literary problem he explored and, with irony, exploited to his own advantage.

Under the influence of Turgenev's fiction Howells rethought the purpose of the novel and once again saw a new direction for himself as a writer. Still restless about his achievement in *A Chance Acquaintance*, he knew that as after *Their Wedding Journey* he again needed a new format. Despite some similarity in theme and characterization, *A Foregone Conclusion* works quite differently from *A Chance Acquaintance*. Critics usually emphasize its more dramatic, less expository quality, but its method of signifying is also different. America has significance, particularly as a goal of Don Ippolito's desire, but is not thematically central. Ferris is an American, but not, like Christopher Newman, defined in national terms, or like Miles Arbuton in regional terms. Florida Vervain is an independent American girl, but not, like Daisy Miller or Isabel Archer, presented as *the* American. That is, characters do not signify geographical areas, nor, as in James's early work, is the novel's focus the international theme.[4] Don Ippolito is not *the* European, nor *the* priest. Howells emphasizes his difference from other priests: he does not spy, he lacks faith, he did not want to be a priest, he tinkers with unpriestly contraptions. His uniqueness is further set off by contrast with the sympathetic Padre Girolamo.

The four main characters are presented through reiterated motifs and manners that manifest Howells' interest in them. Their operating space has a highly charged sexual atmosphere, within which sex both threatens control and motivates action. Sex, in terms of love, lust, and gender distinctions, is in effect the pivot of all of Howells' early works.[5] At the same time, what is remarkably absent from almost all of Howells' early work is money, commerce, capitalism—the most salient factors in the real world he was supposedly reflecting in his fiction. In fact, only in *April Hopes* (1887), a novel often dismissed as an insipid satire of courtship patterns, did he explicitly articulate the connection between capitalism and genteel marriage in America. The novels succeeding *April Hopes*, and influenced by his reading of Tolstoy and socialist theory, then revolved around a series of compromises with an economic system which he ostensibly disliked for its cruelties and its debasement of the writer but on which he depended, paradoxically, for his "success" and the authority which he as a writer-critic had developed. Thus his continuing loyalty to the Republican Party, and thus his fear of militant unionism and of any threateningly strong organization of the other that might undermine the tradition and the classes on which his authority depended, and his fervent hope that the written word would bring forth a peaceful socialist change with continuities to the past.

Until the 1880s, therefore, themes tied to money and power were generally outside Howells' fiction, even as James, whose chosen absence from commercially controlled America allowed him more psychological freedom to maneuver, was able to write fiction which reeks of money. Howells' novels do revolve around a thematics of sex, however, partly because fictional conventions provided numerous tactics for prudently presenting such themes. A writer felt less certainty exploring potentially dangerous economic issues in a period of rapid economic change. The thematics of sex, moreover, are continually connected to control, force, and at times art.

Although Howells provides few explicit links between the courtship surface and figurative readings to authorize such readings, the repetition of certain sexual paradigms throughout his fiction provides some evidence for associating such patterns with underlying social and economic concerns. The intention here is not to argue for such interpretations so much as to explore ways in which an emerging Realist mediated important aspects of the world around him but actually helped create a world he thought he was reflecting.

In *Their Wedding Journey* landscape itself, especially Niagara Falls, is imbued with sexuality, and control of Niagara's force is indicated both by the reiterated marriage motif and by the observer-orderer role of the Marches. Basil's disorganized appearance at the end, however, hardly implies control. In *A Chance Acquaintance* Miles's passion for Kitty is balanced by her desire for what he represents, and both are thematically extended by the regional allegory in which each participates. The intentionally loose ends of the denouement leave not only Kitty's personal future but also the social implications of the struggle for control rather undecided. Like Kitty, Florida Vervain is a physically attractive and independently minded American teenager. She is more arrogant and manipulative than Kitty, less sentimentalized, but also as the sexual center of the book is the magnet to which the other characters are attracted. In *A Chance Acquaintance* Howells can attenuate Kitty's physical features through topical associations of her with the West, which then convey his social themes.

Compare the opening introductions of Kitty and Florida. We learn that Kitty has gray eyes, is pretty, and is romantic. There is no passage like the opening description of Florida:

> She was a girl of about seventeen years, who looked older; she was tall rather than short, and rather full,—though it could not be said that she erred in point of solidity.... She was blonde, with a throat and hands of milky whiteness; there was a suggestion of freckles on her regular face where a quick color came and went, though her cheeks were habitually somewhat pale; her eyes were very blue, under their level brows, and the lashes were even lighter in color than the masses of her fair gold hair; the edges of the lids were touched with the faintest red. (14)

Far more attention is paid to Florida's physical features.[6] Whereas Kitty's childhood and background are quite fully explained, however, Florida's are not. Her peregrinating youth and her late father's heroism against the Seminoles are about all we learn.

Howells uses one figurative device most Realists adopt—signifying names—to establish salient characteristics of his heroine. Both of the names of this fair flower of America, of course, have botanical implications; but they also suggest her hot temper and her pride. "Florida" may also be a reminder of her transient childhood, which keeps her from being identified with New York or Boston society or any particular region even as she is throughly "American," and also of her father whose temperament she inherits. She is also very vain, and her haughtiness is emphasized a dozen times in order to define her character; but her arrogance is also presented as a cover for underlying passion, comparable to Ferris' painting and Ippolito's tinkering as mechanisms of control and sublimation. If her surface pride implies she is unattainable, her passionate outbursts and concern for her mother indicate the opposite. Her sexual significance, moreover, is reinforced by explicit suggestions. As Ferris is arranging a tutor for Florida, Mrs. Vervain warns him that her teachers tend to fall in love with her. A fatherly priest is considered appropriate by both mother and consul, even as Howells himself mixes the message by having Mrs. Vervain make an almost irrelevant reference to Lord Byron. Byron at that time was being discussed in connection with the notorious scandals of Lady Byron's memoirs and their incestuous implications. Ferris himself blocks the inuendos of the scene with a sequence of jokes, a common defense mechanism. Mrs. Vervains's attraction to Fra Girolamo is described as "love at first sight on both sides." Ippolito's invention and personality are, she infers, "one of your jokes"; and Ferris continues with the ironic banter that protects him from involvement.

When he does enlist the priest as a tutor he, again with nervous humor, describes it as a choice between securing "him for Miss Vervain, or for Art—as they call it. Miss Vervain won because she could pay him, and I didn't see how Art could" (37). Of course, he really chooses both, for Ippolito becomes the subject of his best painting. Ferris later tells Ippolito, and thereby misleads him, that he does not love Florida, that he is "the victim of another passion,—I'm laboring under an unrequited affection for Art" (56). His denial is at best, however, circumlocution:

> "Then you do *not* love her?" asked Don Ippolito eagerly.
> "So far as I'm advised at present,—no I don't."
> "It is strange!" said the priest, absently, but with a glowing face.

Ferris is unable to complete the painting of Don Ippolito because he cannot confront himself, because he cannot accept the fact that he has encouraged the priest to assume his own passion. What gives him "a delicious thrill," actually is not Florida's passion but "her willingness to be bidden by him" (60), a trait she too rarely exhibits for him to attain the control he desires. That he achieves only through a sketch of her, which emphasizes hauteur and omits passion. Mrs. Vervain recognizes its one-sideness, and then "the pleasure of the day" deteriorates into a struggle between Ferris' "cold disgust" and Florida's "sudden violence, her visage flaming, and her blue eyes burning upon Don Ippolito."

It is the Don, who is set up not only to fall in love with Florida but also to bear the brunt of her violence, her temperamental outbursts, though they are really intended for Ferris. He with his cool control avoids the heat himself, and only in his absence does Florida's real intent emerge, as when she hurls his hyacinths out the window. Don Ippolito is first introduced as a pathetically ignorant fool, not a sentimental victim as he appears on his deathbed. In his nervous trepidation and anxious uncertainty, he is defined by stupid assumptions that an American consul can procure him a passport, that the United States is at war with South America, and that his clumsily designed cannon would be of interest to the American government. At the same time Howells sets up the Don as a vulnerable figure, he also suggests a sexual situation by having two old gossips whisper that Ippolito "isn't priest enough to hurt the consul," and "would make a very pretty Joseph give him Potiphar's wife in the background."

Ferris meanwhile, unsure how to make use of Ippolito, ungenerously thinks of him with disgust as a "hopeless burden." A young man in the springtime with an eye for "pretty faces," Ferris resists the involvement he seems to seek. Bringing hyacinths to Florida, "who, he fancied, met his attempts at talk with sudden and more than usual hauteur," he resorts to "sulky silence" and the ironically unjust speculation, "'Is she afraid I shall be wanting to make love to her?'" (19). Ferris will not enlist Girolamo as a teacher for the girl whose pride, Howells indicates, is as much Ferris' imagined inference as her own trait, but almost on impulse decides to recruit the poor Don and to watch the humor. Meanwhile the haughty Florida is shown with "strenuous, compassionate devotion" next to her mother and provides the author's own warning that the sympathetic Ferris may be "detestable ... conceited and presuming beyond endurance."

From most writers the sexual implications in scenes with Don Ippolito would inspire substantial commentary; but in Howells criticism they are generally neglected. Ippolito's invention is a breech-loading cannon, one he would turn on the South, even Florida. On the way home it had "broken in his pocket ... by an unlucky thrust ... and the poor toy lay there disabled, as if to dramatize that premature explosion in the secret chamber" (29). He whose name ironically alludes to the son falsely accused of lusting after the father's wife is a rather pagan figure whose anteroom "was painted to look like a grape-arbor ... with many a wanton tendril and flaunting leaf, ... their lavish clusters of white and purple all over the ceiling" (32), like arbors generally seen in front of degenerate palaces and restaurants. His former oratory, now a smithy, had a "sinister effect," as if "invaded by mocking imps, or ... evil powers" searching the forbidden secrets "of the metals and of fire." This pathetically ingenious inventor of useless and unpriestly devices has failed to perfect a mechanism for "steam propulsion," but has made "a few trifles" to offer the ladies. He arrives, however, in an abbate's suit that compromises the Vervains' image of his priestly safeness and implies the irregular feelings in his heart.

Ippolito sings praises of Florida's beauty, receives false confirmation of Ferris' disinterest, and goes home to celebrate and despair at his love. Ferris meanwhile disingenuously wonders "what the priest meant by pumping him in that way. Nothing, he supposed, and yet it was odd" (57). When he learns the truth, he finds that "to his nether consciousness it had been long familiar ... the undercurrent of all his reveries" (122). His outraged reaction to the priest's confession of love for Florida, "'What ... You ... you! A priest?'" is the same as Florida's later shriek, "'*You? A priest!*'" (122, 137). Yet in a sense she has been just as guilty in using Don Ippolito and fostering his advances.

Despite the remorse that occupies both of them, despite Ferris' debauch of hate, jealousy, despair, and guilt, his secular purgatory of the War and penitential wounding, his belated recovery of and marriage to the "angel whose immaculate truth," Ippolito believes, "has mirrored my falsehood in all its vileness and distortion," despite all this Ferris must finally repress all of the Don's threatening emotional significance and remember him merely as a puzzle, a "mere problem" of character. It is at least as much a repression as Florida's portrait. By the end art as well as religious passion have been displaced in a conventional bourgeois marriage. Maimed in the war, Ferris could not paint and was dependent on Florida's money. The Vervains, he once told the Don, could *pay* better than art can.

The significance of all this for Howells' career lay not only in the themes but also in the methods and conventions he was using to develop them. Howells was making dramatically autonomous characters and conflicts vehicles for exploring psychological issues and for disentangling the dilemmas of the artist himself. Seeking to avoid the romantic trappings of Hawthorne and Poe, and the melodrama of Dickens, Howells found in books like *Rudin* and *Smoke* models for using inter-character conflicts to develop social themes.

In *A Chance Acquaintance* Howells set up surface conflict between two principals, and used Dick and Fanny Ellison mostly as a context for Kitty. In *A Foregone Conclusion* he multiplied characters to achieve greater dramatic conflict. Mrs. Vervain bears the same functional relationship to Florida that Fanny does to Kitty, although she is defined more by an innocently scatterbrained class-consciousness than by meddlesome matchmaking. A character like Don Ippolito, however, allows her a larger thematic role, for as he becomes the troublesome "father" she is the difficult mother. Both die before Florida and Ferris can consummate their relationship. Like Basil March, Ferris is a potential artist diverted into a money-making vocation. Like Miles Arbuton he represses passions that may involve him with others. A distinction is also drawn in terms of Ippolito being a (pseudo-) engineer and Ferris an artist. Both serve in official capacities to which they are far less devoted. On the one hand the engineer and the artist were for Howells equivalent images for the writer. In his two early plays one of each is a hero. Both professions provided a way for the self-made western youth to make it in the East. On the other hand they were different, the engineer highly honored in America, the artist less secure. To Don Ippolito America is a country of enterprise, of go-getters; perhaps his inventions will pave the way for him there. American painters, on the other hand, scurry to Europe for instruction and a friendly environment. Ippolito, having lost his religion—"I have no church" (94)—turns his religious drive in the secular direction of America, a country of engineers, embodied then in Florida, who promises him a way to get there. Only when the secular dream is destroyed does he revert to God. Ferris, also a child of an age of doubt, turns to art, but without genius or strength of character. Ippolito's love for Florida contradicts his other dream, and Ferris' sexual drive is set up in opposition to his art.

The same combination of narcissism and non-commitment that prevents Ferris from loving another also restricts his paintings to solipsism. In the novel he does two portraits. In one of these he tries to control, tame, what Florida signifies to him. In the second he paints Don Ippolito, whom all along he has manipulated as a surrogate self who can divert his own religious passion into sexual passion and substitute for Ferris without being a direct threat. Ippolito's necessary failure can still leave Ferris with Florida. Howells meanwhile was able to use the triangular conflict not only to assert the inadequacy of such non-involvement but to explore the writer's—even the Realist's—tendency to see and re-create the Other in terms of what he already knows, in effect to fall prey to solipsism. As Florida and Ferris both realize, the painting of Don Ippolito is in danger of looking only like good old Father O'Brien, or perhaps like an Anypriest. Ferris promises to get all of Venice into the work, to contextualize for particularity and richness. In the end, though, the painting attracts no buyer and as for its subject, it "'isn't just to him; it attributes things that didn't belong to him, and it leaves out a great deal'" (162). Through either ending, the tragic or the comically ironic, Howells defines the problem of the writer who remakes his subject in his own service if not his own image in order to maintain control over forces that threaten his art and his self—whether they are articulated in sexual, social, or economic terms. *A Foregone Conclusion* was Howells' first self-conscious fictional exploration of the problem of authorship, and his only one before 1880.

Notes

1. The letter to Boyesen is included, and the letter to Norton quoted, in W. D. Howells, *Selected Letters*, ed. G. Arms and C. K. Lohmann (Boston: Twayne, 1979) 2:78. Also see the discussion of the issue in Edwin H. Cady, *The Road to Realism* (Syracuse: Syracuse UP, 1956) 188-91. The fullest discussion is John W. Crowley, "'A Completer Verity': The Ending of W. D. Howells' *A Foregone Conclusion*," *English Language Notes* 14 (1977): 192-97.

2. The source of my reference is the text established by David J. Nordloh and David Kleinman for The Library of America in *Novels 1875-1886* (New York, 1982). I am grateful to Professor Nordloh for his help in using the Howells collection at Indiana University.

3. Of course, Ferris and Staniford are separated by less ironic distance from the author than are Arbuton and Easton, so each conclusion does suit the author's fantasies. In *A Chance Acquaintance*, moreover, identification is split between the male Arbuton and the westerner Kitty; and in *Private Theatricals* Howells created his first "pair" of male friends and made the rejected suitor the less attractive and masculine, the other— William Gilbert—having been smitten by the bug but withdrawing after a bitter conflict with Easton. Finally, there are good reasons not to allow the courtship of Miles and Kitty to succeed, reasons essential to theme and structure, regardless of whether the sequence at the end seems unrealistic; and the sexual implications of Belle Farrell's behavior also mandated something short of marriage in the denouement of *Private Theatricals*. There are, however, few reasons why Florida should not marry Ferris or Lydia marry Staniford.

4. The international theme is a dimension of the book, but not a heavily emphasized theme. See the discussion of *A Foregone Conclusion* in Olov W. Fryckstedt, *In Quest of America: A Study of Howells' Early Development as a Novelist* (Cambridge: Harvard UP, 1958).

5. The first critic to explore this topic seriously was Elizabeth Prioleau. See the second chapter of *The Circle of Eros: Sexuality in the Work of William Dean Howells* (Durham, N.C.: Duke UP, 1983).

6. The manuscript shows Howells unsure whether to make Florida seventeen or nineteen.

7. Kenneth Lynn provides useful insights on Ferris in *William Dean Howells: An American Life* (New York: Harcourt Brace Jovanovich, 1971).

6

Roughing It:
Authority Through Comic Performance

When Herman Melville wrote, "Dollars damn me; ... What I feel most moved to write, that is banned,—it will not pay. Yet, altogether, write the *other* way I cannot. So the product is a final hash, and all my books are botches," he was articulating a chronic insecurity of American authors about the audiences for whom they wrote.[1] Serious writers in England seem to have adjusted more readily than their American counterparts to restructuring of author-audience relationships by book marketing, technology, and middle-class ascendancy. Perhaps they did so because for years writers there had been allotted a position with some cultural authority. Dickens, Browning, and Eliot could count on a certain continuing patronage or could reshape a new audience. In America, however, the serious poet or prose writer was more often writing in estrangement from his potential audiences.

Scholars such as Emory Elliott and Eric Sundquist have recently explored the reasons for and manifestations of this problem between the American Revolution and the Civil War. The problem can be seen as a hiatus between authority and authenticity.[2] At mid-century, writers such as Longfellow and Stowe were able to use promotional and marketing resources to achieve a popular domestic success comparable to that of new best-selling romances. Hawthorne and especially Melville, however, despite their greater literary ambition, wrote in either righteous or enigmatic separation from American audiences—behind, as it were, the veils of Bartleby and Parson Hooper. Consequently they continued a pattern of author-reader difficulty in America that had in different ways run from Brown and Brackenridge through Cooper, Simms, and Poe. The absence of an international copyright agreement, moreover, also put serious American writers at a disadvantage. Good English novels could be pirated and reprinted cheaply by American presses, while literate shopkeepers and farmers called on publishers mostly for manuals, guides, agricultural pamphlets, and ephemeral newspapers. Pleas for an American literature at the time were, like requests for new copyright laws, as much an economic lament as a patriotic cheer.

As an entrepreneurial model came to dominate American notions of success, it may have seemed even more difficult for writing to splice authenticity of voice with cultural authority. Emerson's secularized congregation was not for long a usable model after philosophy and social science were professionalized, although the lyceum offered for a while a modest and rather insulated influence for effective speakers. Poetry dried up in America except for such private or unread poets as Dickinson and Melville, and of course the unique presence of Whitman, who himself was often unacceptable until transformed into the more genteel Good Gray Poet. In fiction, Henry James after the War chose an English home rather than confront directly the chasm in America between authenticity and authorial success. William Dean Howells and Samuel Clemens, however, developed widely divergent strategies to reestablish a kind of authority for the writer, and in effect became the first two serious American writers to set out to "make it" according to an entrepreneurial model and to succeed in doing so.[3] They began careers with books in the genre of travel narrative, which had both an intellectual respect lacking in popular fictional forms and also a substantial literary tradition. They developed resources of humor, comedy, and satire to gain perspective on and control over their subject matter. Howells arrived at the right time to convert the editorship of the *Atlantic Monthly* into a position of considerable influence and prestige; Clemens utilized the lecture platform to attain a comparable public position.

Howells, however, sought a representational mode of signification for an age of science, while Clemens eschewed any such quest. Validating a progressive Republican myth of a new middle-class America whose reality resisted Howells' ideal yet provided for his success, Howells ostensibly tried to reduce the gap between fiction and reality. Living the contradictions intrinsic to Howells' myth, Clemens flaunted the gap. Howells' settings, figures, and situations purported to represent actual ones and to be representative of typical categories that could be communicated, interpreted, and understood. Clemens, with his comically outrageous, prefatory assertions that his books have no morals or messages, resisted interpretation as a threat to the authority, the very self of the writer, as a medieval knight would not allow a rival to know his name. Names, in fact, are important in Clemens' work, not for allusive or symbolic reasons but as phenomena. Stories may turn on knowing someone's name, on changing one's name, or on spelling names correctly. The permanent use of a *nom de plume* is not only a marketing device but also a tactic for splitting the protected private self from the advertised performing self.[4]

Both Howells and Clemens were influenced by the theater; but whereas Howells as a novelist often sought to efface himself from his dramatic script, Clemens in fiction was a virtuoso dominating the stage. Through such performances he controlled both audience and subject.[5] His humor is not only a delight for listeners and readers, but also a method for blocking interpretation. He once said his works were sermons; but if, as he also said, he was once attracted to the ministry, it was not for the messages but for the centrality it provided the pastor.[6] If his texts are sermons, their impact lies more in the experience than in the messages, which have invited all sorts of conflicting fantasies. *Huckleberry Finn*, for example, like the nation's Constitution, is a protean document. Its meanings are as varied as meanings of the concept "America," and at times seem a function of a million different readers' notion of "America." Like the Constitution it has been glossed over the years by a large segment of an entire profession, and its author's intentions remain clouded in an astonishing verbal performance.

Roughing It, the first book Clemens set out to write as a book and finished, was a kind of literary manifesto for him and provides the clearest introduction to his performative mode and to the function of humorous and comic devices in controlling audience and subject matter. Like Melville's *Typee* it is a semi-autobiographical travel fiction based on an earlier experience. In each book a young sojourner enters a supposedly primitive world; but whereas *Typee* depends on a nature-culture or primitive-civilized dichotomy, even while rendering problematic the conventional moral value of each term, *Roughing It* undermines the dichotomy itself. In *Roughing It* the primitive rarely appears, and when it does it is inaccessible beneath layers of cultural veneer. In its skeptical empiricism, *Roughing It* undermines the nature/society division on which both the gospel of progress and the noble savage depend. It thereby renders difficult most attempts at interpretation. At the same time, it continually draws attention to language in general and to itself as a specific verbal performance. For a book ostensibly about a trip West, *Roughing It* often reads more like a text with the title, "How I became a writer-lecturer in America and what that means."

The preface establishes a paradoxical relationship with readers. It denies intellectual seriousness by asserting that the "book is merely a personal narrative," not history or philosophy. Its purpose is to "while away an idle hour" not to afflict a reader with science or metaphysics. It intends to have no meaning beyond its story, or so it seems, except that it does include history—of the silver fever, regrettably "a good deal" of historical information. It has, moreover, "wisdom" that "leaks" from the author. So it is, after all, "pretentious history"—asserting the uniqueness of its subject and the special credentials of its recorder; and it is a "philosophical dissertation" claiming only "indulgence" not "justification" at "the hands of the reader."[7] When at the end that philosophy issues in a moral, it is just as paradoxical: stay at home and be diligent, else if you leave you will have to work.[8]

Indulgence not justification is always Mark Twain's strategy: justification is proof, validation, grounding of an argument, or in religious terms the freeing of man from guilt; indulgence is gratification, yielding, or the remission from punishment. Twain the heretic never sought justification but always indulgences. Twain the writer never asked readers to validate his statements, but always to yield to them. A reader who justifies shares authority, a reader who indulges grants authority.

From the beginning, moreover, Twain draws attention to the words of the preface themselves, even as he denies larger meaning to the text. Not only do the opening sentences have carefully balanced clauses and parallel structures, but the second sentence emphasizes a silly alliterative phrase ("variegated vagabondizing") and the preface concludes with egregious wordplay: "information appears to stew out of me naturally, like the precious ottar of roses out of the otter." The preface mixes denials and assertions of meaning, an anti-intellectual humor with sophisticated periods—all drawing attention to the verbal surface itself. By the end, each sentence squints in two directions: "Sometimes it has seemed to me that I would give worlds if I could retain my facts; but it cannot be. The more I caulk up the sources, and the tighter I get, the more I leak wisdom." Depending on whether "retain my facts" implies a memory that might preserve significant data or a limitation on the amount of data thrown into a text, the first sentence can have two different meanings. The second can be either a statement of frustrated self-control, or of the greater meaning that grows from a literary episode whose literal, real-life antecedents are concealed.

Twain often plays such games with readers, as if he is saying, "Indulge me my performance and perhaps wisdom will emerge." *Roughing It* keeps performing that message by referring to itself, by centering language and communication in many episodes, by making the choice of a writing career the pivot of the narrative, by satirizing or parodying literary forms, by embedding a series of narratives whose thematic function is questionable, and by deliberately raising the issue of how the text should be read. Twain provides as many false leads and missed leads as do the silver mines, and various passages of social criticism are themselves undermined elsewhere in the text. In effect, therefore, he not only blocks interpretation of messages but resists decoding, hinders explanation of the very system of signification on which meanings in the text depend.

When the youth leaves Missouri for the West—a youth younger than the narrator and younger than the 24-year-old Sam who accompanied Orion to Nevada (unlike Sam this youth "never had been away from home")—he is, we are told, lured and seduced by the dream of travel.[9]

Or, alternatively, he covets the wealth to be made in the silver mines by which one could "become very rich." He is after adventure or wealth, the strange or the well known. His dream is answered by an offer to be a private secretary, though really the practical young man proposes to stay only three months, after which he plans to "hurry home to business," whatever that might be. The brother's office has majesty, grandeur, distinction—the stuff to be a "hero"; yet Twain, sprinkling in absurdities, also says that the brother might "get hanged or scalped, and have ever such a fine time, and write home and tell us all about it" (43). Such a passage, of course, suggests the youth's naivete; but it also obscures the tone of the text, which might be either serious autobiography or burlesque.

Readers defining the text in terms of a contrast between the primitive and the civilized are given a tempting lead in Chapter 2. The two travelers must discard their formal clothing and enter the West more like Robinson Crusoe. They do retain the federal statutes and an unabridged dictionary—their laws and their language. Highly symbolic, it might seem, as they leave "the States" and feel "an exhilarating sense of emancipation from all sorts of cares and responsibilities" in "the close, hot city" (47). Readers, however, are soon reminded that the statutes are readily available in San Francisco, that the West is not without civilization. On the other hand, later events indicate that both language and law do vary greatly with the environment. Passengers "armed to the teeth" with the guns they assume necessary in the barbaric West are the butt of Twain's satire: their guns do not even shoot straight. Gunplay, however, turns out to be a recognized language in part of the West and a source of social status.

The text dismantles myths, but rarely offers clear alternatives. The desperado Slade turns out to be, for the narrator, a polite gentleman at table. A man whose criminal career can paradoxically be exploited on the side of the law then turns out to be a snivelling, alcoholic coward when brought to justice. None of the images is dismissed, all depend on context. Other expectations—of violent Indians, of finger-tip wealth, of natural beauty—are both denied and fulfilled. California is fascinating but less lovely than New England; Hawaii has its splendors, but also its scorpions, mosquitoes, and tarantulas.[10]

Twain's narrative undermines the very distinctions on which such myths depend. Cooper's Indians are satirized as the "mellow moonshine" of romance. The noble savage is belied by the Goshoot Indians, whose name supplies a convenient pun. Indolent beggars, the Goshoots produce nothing and have less virtue than the "ordinary American negro" (144).[11] They are a degraded inferior people. Then, in the midst of an ironic, anti-primitivist assault on native Americans by "me, a disciple of Cooper and worshiper of the Red Man" (146), Twain compares the Goshoots with the

Baltimore and Washington Railroad Company. A chapter asserting the Indians' inferiority to every other race in the world now suggests not only that the white man's railroad has a "plausible resemblance" but also that the very comparison injures "the reputation" of the Rocky Mountain Goshoots. "If we cannot find it in our hearts to give those poor naked creatures our Christian sympathy and compassion, in God's name let us at least no throw mud at them" (147). The Goshoots can have his pity, for nearer by "they never get anybody's." The white railroad men are inferior, and their treatment of the Goshoots reprehensible. On the other hand, the "scholarly savages" of American romance are a lie.[12]

A cultural form is undermined, a political point is made, but the author's overall message is mixed. Earlier chapters on Mormonism demystify, in a similar way, the spiritual pilgrims by showing Brigham Young as a lecherous tyrant and the average Mormon as an exploitable ignoramus. At the same time Twain criticizes Americans and American governments for cruel persecution, and leaves in tension a series of contradictory images of the Mormons. In part he does this by framing other narratives—Johnson's tale of Young's many wives, Street's account of Young's honest treatment of gentile contractors, and the appendices on Mormon history and the Mountain Meadows massacre.[13] Like Cooper's romances, moreover, the Book of Mormon is for Twain an unreliable and pretentious text. Such lying books—like the Bible—that pretend to truth cause much misery. Better to pretend to lie, and let truth leak out.

Verbal structures and literary forms are made problematic from the beginning, as a consequence of the author's retreat from straightforward discursive statements. Language itself is more often a central theme than the clear sign of a represented world. The first character met along the way is the garrulous "Sphynx" who, once the "fountains of her great deep" are opened up, spews forth a flood of gossip, a "tossing waste of dislocated grammar and decomposed pronunciation" (49), that may signify nothing but is in itself enough to change the brothers' itinerary. The embedded tale of the Syrian camel eating Twain's overcoat signifies, if anything in this context, the material value of verbal material. To the camel the pocketed journalistic documents—with their "solid wisdom"— are undigestible viands, fatal *in fact* though in *meaning* "one of the mildest and gentlest statements ... I ever laid before a trusting public" (46). As Twain and his brother ride west atop their dictionary, somewhat interested in "the characters," they stop at a station and are introduced to the western idiom, "the vigorous vernacular of the occidental plains and mountains." This hyperbolic definition satirizes both the pretensions of eastern language and the ultimately "monotonous" nature of actual western speech. "Pass the bread, you son of a skunk!" (63), or some comparable oath "too strong for print," is one of many comments calling into question the realism of printed texts.

Each early chapter foregrounds language as theme in some way, and the pattern continues, for example, in the description of gunplay as communication in Carson City, in Mr. Ballou's ostentatious use of big words, and in a series of episodes centering around the *Enterprise* in Virginia. The Scotty Briggs episode is pivotal in the development of this theme. An eastern preacher's difficulty communicating about a funeral with a western rough not only provides a brilliant performance but renders language a *problem* for truth not the sign of truth. In Nevada such "phrases as 'You bet!' 'Oh, no, I reckon not!' 'No Irish need apply,' and a hundred others, became so common as to fall from the lips of a speaker unconsciously ... when they did not touch the subject under discussion and consequently failed to mean anything" (298).

Scotty's visit to the minister is but one of many interpolated anecdotes in *Roughing It*. Often their importance is less that of exempla of a moral statement than something more ambiguous. The anecdote of the Syrian camel is rather tenuously connected to the mule's taste for sagebrush, but perhaps more related to the problems of language itself. The irreverent tale of Jack, the unlettered New York boy at the grave of Moses, makes no sense in relation to Ben Holliday the stagecoach manager, despite the narrator's claims, but much sense in relation to authority, social classes, and western grammar.[14] The fable of the despised coyote and the confident swift-footed dog may be a naturalist's essay, like that on the jackass and the sagebrush, or a beast fable. The hero is "a living, breathing allegory of Want ... always poor, out of luck and friendless" (66-67). The town-dog and slinking, deceitful coyote seem like Twain's earlier Dandy and Squatter: a shrewd western bushwhacker outsmarts a cocky sophisticate. But if the reader pushes such an allegory very far, perhaps prompted by Twain's comparison of himself with a Brobdingnagian among Lilliputian gnats and ants, he lands where the town-dog lands, "solitary and alone in the midst of a vast solitude" (68). Unless Twain be the coyote and we the dogs, it all leads nowhere.[15]

The comical Hyde-Morgan landslide case provides Twain an excuse for his usual attacks on juries and the judicial process.[16] Since the entire episode, however, is a practical joke in the form of a tall tale, interpretation of the performance as statement is undermined. The subsequent story of Ned Blakely's vigilante justice, moreover, provides a dubious alternative to an imperfect jury system. The mode of the text allows Twain to assert conflicting propositions and still maintain authority and credibility.

Jim Blaine's story of his grandfather's ram is a shaggy dog tale but also an attack on interpretation. Not only does it omit any signified for the ram, it hides or indefinitely defers the signifier. Thereby it leaves control in the hands of Blaine, and Twain himself as the town-dog "in the midst of a vast solitude," at least until he can use and resignify the anecdote in *Roughing It*. Similarly the story of Horace Greeley and Hank Monk signifies nothing allegorically as told but as repeated within the text hyperbolically articulates the life-and-death significance of the performer's authority. To save his sanity, Twain, by now a "melancholy wreck," finally insists that one poor wanderer not be allowed to reiterate the tale. The invalid, crushed by the strain of silence, dies "in our arms" (152). Again the chapter does not merely narrate such a factitious sequence taking place, but forces the reader—like listeners in halls where Twain tried the joke—to live through the performance. The author not only controls his own audience but also controls the earlier texts he incorporates. He resignifies each telling as part of a new structure, just as all the embedded newspaper passages take on new significance when Twain interpolates them in various chapters.

Early in the text, George Bemis' buffalo hunt exemplifies use of the tall tale to preserve authority and resist interpretation. Out of the disgrace of actual failure, Bemis fashions a successful vicarious performance.[17] Ask the liar for justification and, since you have not been there and he has laid claim to his own imaginative space, he can respond:

> "Proofs! Did I bring back my lariat?"
> "No."
> "Did I bring back my horse?"
> "No."
> "Did you ever see the bull again?"
> "No."
> "Well, then, what more do you want? I never saw anybody as particular as you are about a little thing like that." (79)

Rather, grant him his indulgence; and emulate him, says Twain, now assuming his own voice to tell the incredible story of Eckert's coconut-eating Siamese cat. By the end of that tale, Bascom, the skeptical rationalist, is silenced, but not Twain, who can grind "out lies like a mill" (80). By the time one gets to the story of Gridley and his often sold flour sack, the boundary between fact and fiction collapses under the strain of authorial performance.

The concern with authority, true and false, recurs throughout the book, as the youth overcomes ignorance. False authorities like Brigham Young, Captain Cook, and the U. S. Government are unmasked. The bully "Arkansas" is broken, not by physical force but by the superior rhetoric of Mrs. Johnson.[18] A truer authority is held by coach drivers, heroes to the West. Unlike the more powerful conductors, representatives of owners, the drivers are actual performers dominating "the stage" like Twain himself. Meanwhile the youth has proven himself unable to mine for profit and continually vulnerable to a sharp horse trader. A man who is such a bad horse trader should go into writing, for there he can turn failures into successes. Even at the end of the book he is the victim of a practical joke that costs him health and money, but that he converts into a final performance.[19]

The decision to turn to writing is described as a response to failure. On the other hand, the narrator almost wills his failure to make money from the mines. Needing but one day of squatting to assure ownership of the promising Wild West Company lead, the narrator is diverted by his humanitarian concern for the rheumatic Captain Nye:

> It reads like a wild fancy sketch, but the evidence of many witnesses, and likewise that of the official records of Esmeralda District, is easily obtainable in proof that it is a true history. I can always have it to say that I was absolutely and unquestionably worth a million dollars, once, for ten days. (264)

Thus "What to do next?," the opening passage of the second half of *Roughing It.* After a catalog of the dozen or so occupations at which he has failed, the narrator says he "discarded the revolver" (267) and took up the pen. Turning failure into success through writing becomes the motif. Making money becomes easy, because as writer he need not merely report on the value of mines, he can "create" it, though occasionally he has to "patch up" his reputation for accuracy. The first lesson he learns is how to lie and tell the truth at the same time, and how to convert ignorance into power. If towns grant authority to those who kill their man or find their lead, they also must to those who "report" and therefore "create" what is known about them.

Some verbal performances are tied to drunkenness, which puts a man outside himself, sets up an "Other" distinguished from the social self, as Twain was from Clemens. The mild dissolute stranger in Virginia, perhaps Clemens himself, writes when drunk the most outrageous parts of the team-written romance. Jim Blaine must be drunk to perform the tale of the grandfather's ram. On the stage to California, a "seedy-looking vagabond" puts on a performance to bilk a sympathetic crowd of brandy, and then, as if Twain were merely establishing drunken surrogates for himself, the narrator is reminded of another story of a drunk telling yet another story, "'Ye Modest Man Taketh a Drink.' It was nothing but a bit of acting, but it seemed to me a perfect rendering, and worthy of Toodles himself." Subsequently "another gentleman present told about another drunken man," and by the end a battery of narratives have been performed (361). Through the rest of the book control by verbal performance remains the only constant. The tall tale of Dick Baker's cat Tom Quartz, blown sky-high by dynamite and returning only a bit sooty; the factitious histories of the "Admiral" and passenger Williams; the grand printed program for Princess Victoria's funeral—all center performance and rhetoric.

What does it all "mean" beyond what it says? Perhaps that is best answered by the puzzling response an eccentric Michigan preacher receives from Horace Greeley when he asks how to "make of the turnip a climbing vine" (450). Even then the preacher, like a critic, is but an intermediary, for Widow Beazeley of Campbellton, Kansas. Greeley's letter, like Twain's text, resists decoding. Simple Simon Erickson tries four different interpretations, all coherent if silly, and drives himself mad in the rage for meaning. When Greeley's second letter clears up the ambiguity, it does not save the widow's son, nor make turnips aspire upwards, nor really replace the holograph version, which has on it exactly the same words. Not in the meaning of the words but in the performance of them and the experience of reading them lies the text.

If Twain is in one sense Greeley, however, he is in another *Markiss*, the insufferable liar who haunts the narrator on the island of Maui. A man whose presence makes the narrator so uncomfortable he would prefer to "enjoy a missionary" with some cannibals, Markiss pops up like a conscience whenever Twain is telling a story that veers from the factual.[20] When discovered as a suicide some years later, he cannot even be declared dead, for to do so would be to accept his presentation of his (dead) self as valid, whereas "whatever statement he chose to make was entitled to instant and unquestioning acceptance as a *lie*" (491). As writer, that is, Twain establishes authority by being Greeley; one cannot control his texts through decoding and interpretation. He also is Markiss, whose essential self baffles all conventional truth tests (except "mental aberration"). He is the destroyer of false gods, but like the missionaries ready to reeducate those whose gods have been destroyed. He is the poseur of ignorance and failure, but the monarch of all he surveys. At a time when his new friend Howells was developing a literary mode with signifying authority worthy of an age of science, Clemens was developing a mode that could thrive on internal contradictions and undermine signification itself, that through the lecture platform or the printed book could establish authority in the performance itself and literary value in the experience of reading a text not in the meaning extracted from the text.

Notes

1. *The Letters of Herman Melville*, ed. M. R. Davis and W. R. Gilman (New Haven: Yale UP, 1960) 128.

2. Emory Elliott, *Revolutionary Writers: Literature and Authority in the New Republic, 1725-1810* (New York: Oxford UP, 1982); Eric J. Sundquist, *Home as Found: Authority and Genealogy in Nineteenth-Century American Literature* (Baltimore: Johns Hopkins UP, 1979). Also see the insightful readings of Hawthorne by John Franzosa, for example,

"The Language of Inflation in 'Rappaccini's Daughter,'" *Texas Studies in Literature and Language* 24 (1982): 1-22.

3. On Twain's concern with authenticity, see Everett Emerson, *The Authentic Mark Twain: A Literary Biography of Samuel L. Clemens* (Philadelphia: U of Pennsylvania P, 1984).

4. The most thorough study of Twain's creation of a public personality distinct from his private self is Louis J. Budd, *Our Mark Twain: The Making of His Public Personality* (Philadelphia: U of Pennsylvania P, 1983).

5. A rather insightful study of *Roughing It* that does attend to its quality of performance is Chapter 6 of Warwick Wadlington, *The Confidence Game in American Literature* (Princeton: Princeton UP, 1975). He is good on Twain's "flexible authorial marginality," his active utilization of the narrative persona, his dependence on and play with cultural conventions, and the importance of an implied audience to the text.

6. On 31 July 1906, Twain wrote: "I have always preached. That is the reason that I have lasted thirty years. If the humor came of its own accord and uninvited, I have allowed it a place in my sermon, but I was not writing the sermon for the sake of the humor" (*Mark Twain in Eruption*, ed. Bernard DeVoto [New York: Harper, 1922] 202). In a letter of 19-20 October 1865, he wrote to Orion and Mollie that his only powerful ambitions had been to be a pilot and a preacher. He could not be the latter for want of religion. The letter will be included in the new University of California edition of Twain's letters. I thank the editors of the Mark Twain Papers, Bancroft Library, for access to this and related materials.

7. Mark Twain, *Roughing It*, vol. 2 in *The Works of Mark Twain*, ed. Franklin R. Rogers and Paul Baender (Berkeley: U of California P, 1972) 28. Further references are included in the text.

8. Philip Beidler reads the prefaces of Twain's early works more straightforwardly. See "Realistic Style and the Problem of Context in *The Innocents Abroad* and *Roughing It*," *American Literature* 52 (1980): 33-49. Beidler discusses *Roughing It* as a book about writing in which Twain learns from the experiences of others about the nature and importance of expression.

9. The standard discussion of the relationship between author, narrator, and tenderfoot in *Roughing It* is Henry Nash Smith, "Mark Twain as an Interpreter of the Far West: The Structure of *Roughing It*," in *The Frontier in Perspective*, ed. Walker D. Wyman and Clifton B. Kroeber (Madison: U of Wisconsin P, 1957) 205-28. Much background information is included in Martin B. Friend, "The Sources, Composition, and Popularity of Mark Twain's *Roughing It*" (Diss. University of Chicago 1951).

10. Franklin R. Rogers has explored Twain's imaginative fusion of two stock characters from burlesque travel literature—the sentimentalist and the realist. He shows that a new point of view is thereby created, that of the post-war American adjusting to new realities. See "The Road to Reality: Burlesque Travel Literature and Mark Twain's *Roughing It*," *Bulletin of the New York Public Library* 67 (1963): 155-68.

11. The usual spelling was Gosiute, "a contraction of Go-ship or Gossip, the name of a former chief combined with the tribal name *Ute*" (Franklin R. Rogers, "Explanatory Notes" to *Roughing It*, p. 566). Rogers also comments on Twain's deliberate exaggeration of the tribe's degradation.

12. Helen L. Harris persuasively argues that Twain's white chauvinism leads him generally to condone injustices to Indians. On the other hand, Twain can always invert one criticism to establish another and play both angles simultaneously, as with Colonel Sherburn and his cowardly lynch mob, or Senator Dilworthy and his constituents who truly deserve him. See Harris, "Mark Twain's Response to the Native Americans," *American Literature* 46 (1975): 495-505.

13. The appendices were not included in the English edition.

14. This anecdote was originally written in May 1868 and set up in the form of a letter to the editor of a San Francisco newspaper. It will be included in the third volume of the *Early Tales and Sketches* (Iowa-California Edition). Out of the present context it works rather differently.

15. Henry Nash Smith argues that this episode epitomizes the book's central themes (*Mark Twain: The Development of a Writer* [Cambridge: Belknap Press of Harvard UP, 1962] 54-56). Two more recent articles that put disillusion or self-contempt at the center of the book are Tom H. Towers, "'Hateful Reality': The Failure of the Territory in *Roughing It*," *Western American Literature* 9 (1974): 3-15; and Forrest G. Robinson, "'Seeing the Elephant': Some Perspectives on Mark Twain's *Roughing It*," *American Studies* 21 (1981): 43-64.

16. See Franklin Rogers' explanatory note in *Roughing It*, pp. 580-81. The episode was first published as a separate hoax-story, "The Facts in the Great Land Slide Case," in the Buffalo *Express* 2 April 1870.

17. James M. Cox argues that the Bemis story illustrates the themes of tale telling and the truth that can exist in lies (*Mark Twain: The Fate of Humor* [Princeton: Princeton UP, 1966] 100-04). Wadlington, revising Cox's reading, suggests that the complete skeptic is shown to be just as vulnerable as the naif (*Confidence Game* 204-05).

18. See the original version of this episode, a partial dramatization drafted most likely in 1870 (*Roughing It* 536-41). The heroes who put the

bully "Arkansaw" in his place, physically not rhetorically, are Scotty Briggs and Buck Fanshaw, not the barkeep's wife.

19. Twain fictionalizes the account of his first lecturing experience in San Francisco, borrowing from Irving's *Life of Goldsmith*. See Paul Fatout, "Mark Twain's First Lecture: A Parallel," *Pacific Historical Review* 25 (1956): 347-54.

20. In Twain's notebook such a person is named F. A. Oudinot. It is not clear how much of the chapter is totally invented.

7

The Gilded Age:
Performance, Power, and Authority

The Gilded Age is Mark Twain's most Dickensian work. Full of grotesque originals like Colonel Sellers, who is often compared with Mr. Micawber, the novel is a mixture of realism and fable. It criticizes bureaucracy, plutocracy, corruption, and human cruelty. In part a parody of sentimental and sensational imitations of Dickens, it nonetheless depends on the same qualities of performance and manipulation of audience that Dickens so fully developed. Although ambivalent towards Dickens' fiction, Twain did not consistently condemn it in the way he did the fiction of Austen, Eliot, and James. To some extent he may have realized that he was working in a tradition that included Rabelais, Cervantes, Swift, and Dickens himself, and that thrived not on representation or reflection but on authorial performance and creation of a fictive world at some remove from reality. Unlike Dickens, however, Twain avoided contemporary settings for his fiction, which is generally set either in a distant European past or on the Mississippi River of his ante-bellum childhood. The Sellers novels are exceptions, and perhaps because *The Gilded Age* takes place largely in post-Civil War America Twain most fully frees it from the fetters of realism. Out of frontier tall tales and Dickensian exaggeration, he creates a world loosely corresponding to social reality but vividly suggesting real American fantasies.

To develop this world Clemens uses several tactics. He opens with a preface and first chapter that are full of incongruities and pull the book away from representational conventions. He counterpoints his own histrionic chapters against Charles Dudley Warner's straighter romance, which provides an alternative voice and motifs that can be played for thematic parallels even while being burlesqued. He deploys his characters in performances that are vehicles of satire but also phenomena in a Barnum extravaganza. The methods, audiences, and success of the performances become as significant as their themes.

81

Bryant Morey French and other scholars have provided detailed keys to the political satire and literary parody in *The Gilded Age*, though it might be added that the book has more literary than political sophistication.[1] Like Henry Adams, in *Democracy*, Clemens attributed America's problems to corrupt Congressmen and fundamental human greed and weakness. Power was generally in Washington, not on Wall Street. Business abuses took place outside of established and reputable corporations. Middle-class Americans, of course, seemed willing to believe that the crash of 1873 was due to Jay Cooke's broken promises and that other injustices were due to cases of individual corruption.[2] At a relatively chaotic time economically, moreover, Americans were persuaded that the cathartic mechanisms of competition were superior to public accountability, regulation, and reform. The system itself was sound. Clemens himself in 1873 understood business corruption and political corruption, but had less sense of the problems posed by legitimized power in America.

He did perceive a discontinuity between discourse and fantasy in America—a gap between a language of democracy and aristocratic aspirations, a gap between dreams and moral values tied to the land and a social system in which land—like self—had value only as commodity, a gap between a myth of a transcendent self and a society in which marketing, costuming, and managing self were what counted. Clemens did have a personal investment, of course, in not fully understanding the contradictions of business enterprise and the self-made man, for his own literary authority depended on success along the lines of those models, and in not fully understanding his own complicity in the discontinuities between discourse and fantasy that he was exposing. As he undermined current forms of economic, political, and cultural power, moreover, he also defined a model of survival and success through performance in which a "real" self is effaced by the performer's mask.

While *Roughing It* is a portrait of the writer as a young man, purporting to be a travel book of the West, *The Gilded Age* is a fantasy of the writer's authority presenting itself as political satire and literary parody. In *Roughing It* performance is a resolution of the writer's difficulty, but in *The Gilded Age* it is the central theme or problem. Economic motives, systems, and codes are displaced by rhetorical and performative systems. In the end persons act less out of economic self-interest than out of their fantasies as energized by theater and rhetoric. Even sex is a vulnerable system of control. When Selby reappears, Laura, often successful at dramatically exploiting her sexuality, cannot control through her performer's mask her "real" and sexual self. Lacking the skills of Sellers, Dilworthy, and Twain, she dies after failure on the lecture platform, a projection of the fear that in *Roughing It* Twain implies haunted him before his first public success.

As in *Roughing It*, an opening preface immediately defamiliarizes readers and establishes an authority separate from referentiality. The author disclaims "usual" reasons for writing a book—hardly usual in fact—and therefore the need for one of those "usual apologies." Such an apology, of course, follows. Contradicting the sub-title, "A Tale of To-Day," he then insists the book "deals with an entirely ideal state of society" lacking illustrative models in the everyday world.[3] The sophomoric lies of the next sentence—that "there is no fever of speculation, no inflamed desire for sudden wealth" and that the poor all are contented and the rich are all generous in America—continue to authorize a skeptical attitude toward the letter of the text. The epigraphs—those "attractive scraps of literature"—come in many languages as part of a strategy not to write for one nation "but to take in the whole world," Twain's most candid statement of his underlying purpose.

The first chapter continues to treat language as a problem not as a vehicle of truth. Amid a rural wasteland suggesting George Washington Harris' frontier humor, *Squire* Hawkins is "contemplating the morning," phrasing a bit incongruous with setting but nonetheless soon repeated.[4] The poorest white class accepts one family as "the quality." Then through a language even more out of place, the Squire weaves fantasies of new wealth. The exaggerated backwoods dialect of the farmers is in contrast with the melodramatic cliches of Hawkins' dreams and with his dialogue with Nancy so as to imply a certain myopia. Meanwhile the certainty or determinacy of the narrator's own messages is undermined by a series of sentences such as the following: "The district ... had a reputation like Nazareth, as far as turning out any good thing was concerned."[5]

The American Dream indicated is precariously balanced between land and money. Hawkins invests in a piece of Tennessee property that is to assure his children's future. As America shifted from an agricultural to an industrial economy, real estate or commodification of land was the first source of wealth. The internal contradictions of a society whose myths remained agrarian and therefore irrelevant to new conditions are suggested by the Hawkinses' intent to make an "extravagant fortune" from their land while being reluctant to let it go. Ostensibly held for a higher price, it becomes a talisman irrationally preserved from commercial exchange as the family struggles with the cruelties of a speculative economy. Once the basis of status and family, land now has only the exchange value of any other commodity. Its value, moreover, one infers from *The Gilded Age* may depend largely on political corruption.

To Squire Hawkins "there's oceans of money in that land," and the family's sucess will be marked by its millionaires and its governors and the reputation of the name Hawkins. The land, however, turns out to be the primary symbol of his paternal failure. *The Gilded Age* is the first of a series of novels that illustrate Clemens' deep-seated concern with bad or absent fathers, a concern as much related to his own obsession with dominance and authority as to problems from his youth. The romantic dreams of Hawkins lift him out of the squalor of his Tennessee neighbors, but also make him vulnerable to the promises of Colonel Sellers.

Actually his naive hopes project Sellers as an aspect of Hawkins' own personality, of his own fantasies. Contemplating the morning, at his "double log cabin, in a state of decay," Hawkins receives a letter from Sellers, who emerges, as it were, out of his own consciousness, and who is, conversely, to the more practical Nancy "a shadow" blurring the sunlight, "a procession of disturbing thoughts that began to troop through her mind." A force drawing Hawkins—as Clemens' own father had been drawn—from Virginia to Kentucky to Tennessee to Missouri, Sellers has personal traits drawn from Clemens' relative James Lampton. His particular ventures, however—cornering the slave trade, engineering a perpetual motion machine, exploiting a new fossil fuel—connect him with a more broadly representative American experience. Suitably he is soon at work on a scheme tied to the railroads. Like the narrator himself, moreover, Sellers has "the biggest scheme on earth—and I'll take you in; I'll take in every friend I've got...." (21).

After the adoption of Laura and the introduction of Sellers, the theme of success is developed in conjunction with a search for a substitute father, a more adequate or at least more convincing model for a period in which "history finds certain changes to record" (49). Young George Washington, sent to live at the Sellers home, takes the Colonel as a new father, fitting his own impractical visions to Sellers' speeches, "growing opulent under the magic of his eloquence," and "building glittering pyramids of coin." In fact, "he could have worshiped that man" (71). Laura's parentage is part of the book's melodrama, a parody of contemporary fiction. When her problem is left unresolved, Clemens apologizes for the loose end; but by recalling the issue in his epilogue, he in a sense confirms that Laura did find a father—Dilworthy. He initiates her into American politics, sets up her successful performances, and takes care of her in his home—all to capitalize on the Tennessee land. Dilworthy instructs Laura in what she needs to know. In guarding her against inappropriate advances, he counsels, "My daughter, ... I trust there was nothing free in his manner.... There, there, child. I meant nothing" (265). Although she does not call him Father, more than once she calls him Uncle (263, 266, 321). In the gilded age, the America of Laura and Washington Hawkins, Sellers and Dilworthy are the paternal models for ambitious youth. They survive because they are creations of American desire, not merely exploiters of innocent victims.

Sellers and Dilworthy are faces of the same figure, although critics emphasize their differences.[6] One embodies the speculative mania of westward migration, mining fortunes, and the railroad, that is economic power. The other embodies a related desire for political power through "democracy." In a sense, Dilworthy replaces Sellers when management, consolidation, and incorporation replace expansion and dream as the mode of American desire. When Dilworthy visits Hawkeye, he begins to replace Sellers as the symbolic center of the text. Sellers, in fact, fancies that he himself has hosted and sponsored the popular politician; and the text implies a moral similarity between the ante-bellum pro-slavery values of Sellers and Dilworthy's post-war exploitation of the freedmen's cause and saccharine piety.[7]

Sellers dominates the first half of the book, largely through a series of monologues. With the rhetoric of promotional tracts, he offers paternal protection to the Hawkins family or to young George Washington. Through verbal performance he also creates an imaginary world out of whatever is absent in his actual world. A bizarre dysfunctional clock, a stove warmed by a lone candle, a dinner of turnips and water all become through his magical eloquence the keys to health and success, like the Tennessee land. In one scene Sellers boasts of his "prodigious operations"—bossing the market in corn, speculating on hogs, buying up wildcat banks, and making millions from patented eyewash. Like his earlier ventures, together they suggest a compendium of American dreams, a new deal for young George Washington, fatherly advice for one himself named after the father of his country. In St. Louis, Napoleon, and Hawkeye, Sellers can speak just as persuasively of western lands, railroading, and town development, so that the desires and dreams of young engineers and profiteers are fulfilled before they even set forth.

In these sequences Sellers' domesticity is emphasized, his paternal guidance of both his own large brood and a series of young hopefuls like Washington Hawkins, Harry Brierly, and Philip Sterling. Secondly, in these performances Sellers is unconscious of any hypocritical gap between his language and the world to which it refers. He assimilates his mask completely. Nancy cannot help but like him, Si cannot help but believe him, and Harry and Philip follow him. If not integrity his performance has internal coherence. Sellers, in creating not reflecting a reality, has authority over it and over an indulgent audience of whose own desires he is a projection. His presence in Hawkeye when Harry and Philip arrive personifies their own ambition even more than it reflects the kind of village tout to be found in such places at that time. Sellers also survives because he seems to have no underlying, non-performing, "real" self making him vulnerable. When unpaid railroad workers storm the Navigation Office at Stone's Landing, his golden tongue pacifies the mob and makes of them all "rich men" with "a lot in the suburbs of the city" though they "had no money and nothing to live on" and "his family spent their days in poverty" (192). In his absence they can promise to hang him; present and performing, he has authority and control.

In the nation's capital, however, Clemens uses Sellers inconsistently. When he and Washington discuss Congressional investigations of corruption, Sellers does not make empirically untrue statements that create a self-contained "truth" but rather makes empirically true statements from an immoral perspective (380-83). While Clemens uses this scene to indicate some maturity on the part of Washington Hawkins, he allocates more moral self-consciousness to Sellers than elsewhere in the text. Dilworthy not Sellers, however, dominates this part of the story. Usually read as an incorrigible hypocrite to Sellers' lovable buffoon, he is not *within the text* described as conscious of any hypocrisy. Based on the notorious Senator Pomeroy of Kansas, and more generally on venal post-war politicians, he is still never presented as aware of a gap between his mask and a real self.[8] Readers justifiably interpret him in relation to villains more conscious of their falsity, but as a kind of Dickensian grotesque he is not particularly bound by verisimilitude. Discussing Senators Balloon and Hopperson with Laura, Dilworthy never once drops his mask (263, 265), even though the subtext of their dialogue is crude political coercion.

The only hint of conscious deception is, when Laura enters his room, a Bible upside down in his hands, a prop too hastily added to his costume. Laura herself, in fact, marvels at his ingenuous behavior, she who "knew quite as much of Washington life as Senator Dilworthy gave her credit for, and more than she thought proper to tell him" (266). Buckstone and Trollop, more realistically drawn, are openly conscious of their perfidy. Dilworthy, whether in Hawkeye speaking of patriotism, piety, and racial equity, or in Cattleville addressing Sunday School children, mouths sincerely a gospel he has fully assimilated. His counterattack on honest Mr. Noble is grounded in this same bizarre sincerity. Although reporters, a village drunk in Hawkeye, and the "minority of honest men" in Congress know Dilworthy's guilt, by the end of *The Gilded Age* "truth" is a paltry thing, perhaps inseparable from its production in speaking and writing.

Whereas the first half of the book belongs to Sellers and young men seeking their fortune, the second half belongs to Dilworthy and Laura, converting performance into power. Like *Roughing It*, that is, *The Gilded Age* has two acts—the first presenting attempts to make one's fortune by going West, the second focusing on language, writing, and performance as alternative routes to power. In addition to performances aimed at achieving power in Washington, it suggests the potential and limitations of such verbal mediators of experience as books, newspapers, and lectures. While Twain himself continues as performer-author, he satirizes a society in which performance is the route to success. Whether parvenus like the O'Rileys, adopting a new name to assure new status, or politicians like Trollop and Buckstone, or speculators, or women lobbyists, all those who make it need the right stuff, a mask they can exploit for advancement and that effaces any real and more vulnerable self.

In Laura's new world, fabrication and marketing of self are keys to success. Petroleum helps the Gashlys turn from homely rustics into "ornaments of the city." A saloon and ward politics transform Patrick O'Riley into a wealthy Frenchman, Hon. Mr. Oreille, "still bearing the legislative 'Hon.,' attached to his name (for titles never die in America, although we do take a republican pride in poking fun at such trifles)" (249). If his readers do not get the point, Twain has shifted into dramatic dialogue with speech prefixes to emphasize the theatricality of it all.[9] In this world Laura learns to be "the Duchess" and "the reigning belle," "highly educated" daughter "of a distinguished Western family," "a great landed heiress" (238-40). With each retelling her story expands so that although "she still bore the name of Laura Hawkins ... she was perceptibly changed" and grievously uncertain herself "what manner of woman she was" (258). The quality of the performance, in which everyone willingly takes part, determines her acceptance.

With this foundation she can exploit sex to political advantage. For all of Buckstone's awareness of her wiles, her "carefully-contrived artifices and stratagems of war," she controls him. She controls Trollop, moreover, largely because she gets in a position to work on his speeches, to control the language he uses. Unlike Dilworthy and Sellers, however, Laura is openly cognizant of her hypocrisy, has not fooled herself into equating the national good and her personal good. Retaining her previous romantic self, still seeking true love and passion, "urged on by a fever of love and hatred and jealousy," she is vulnerable to the weaknesses of that self (297). Selby's reappearance not only leads to her demise but even more quickly destroys the social position she has built up through performance: "she had lost character with the best people" (327).[10]

If Sellers and Dilworthy are projections of American desire, Laura embodies that desire and its frightening consequences. Her orphan background with its mystery of ancestry, her dream of wealth and status, her betrayal by her own romantic ideas, and her quest for restitution through democratic government all ironically tie her to American experience, while her name links her to a romantic episode in Twain's own youth.[11] Her real, vanquished, vulnerable self stands before an audience, unable to convert her failure into platform success as Twain himself had. The real self has less potential for authority and power than does a mask that can help transform experience into fictional performance. People, Twain said, do not listen to truth directly, but only through lies and poses; by indirection it sometimes seeps through.

Those most bent on direct revelation are Congressmen like Noble, destroyed in the attempt, and Newspaper Row. Battling their own cynicism, reporters record particulars of Washington corruption. Depending mostly on rumors and gossip and leaks from Sellers (of all people), however, they can hardly pretend to truth. They are more "true" when satirizing Senator Balloon for misuse of the franking privilege than when reporting facts of legislative action. Stories of the murder and Laura's trial vary widely, despite the best intentions, for they do not so much report as create the truth. "Colored and heightened by the reporters' rhetoric" and "sympathy for the poor girl" and "improvement" by the leading journals, the stories fit data into literary prototypes or fit data to political biases (351-53). While *The Gilded Age* parodies conventional sensational romances, and other forms in which formula governs fact, it also suggests that satire or parody or any discourse that writes against convention has more chance of significant authority than does an attempt at representation. The problems of mediating experience, moreover, do not end with the printed page, for in a world in which literature is a commodity, marketing may be the crucial literary process. Laura's experience in a bookstore indicates that few distributors, in Twain's eyes, know "about literature *as* literature, in contradistinction to its character as merchandise" (274).

Justice, like politics in *The Gilded Age*, is only obliquely related to truth. Since juries, like electorates, are established on the basis of ignorance and incompetence, a tear-jerking performance by Lawyer Braham is more significant than real evidence. In an adversarial jury system, after all, victory, not truth, is the goal.

Final arbiter of his own text, Twain flaunts his control in the scene following Laura's trial. After narrating her confinement in an asylum, he withdraws that "beautiful" incident "which no fiction-writer would dare imagine, a scene of touching pathos, creditable to our fallen humanity" (427). Inconsistently saying that it is actually an ending from "a work of fiction," he then imposes an ending for "history and not fiction," thereby paradoxically reminding his readers that this is fiction, not history. In earlier comments that novels are not real life (276) and that it is "impossible for the historian ... to control events or compel the persons of his narrative" (371), Twain signifies his control over the performance. The many if's dotting Chapter 50 propose alternative routes for a fictional text, not futile speculations on history. Because "there is no such law or custom" (429) for reality as for "true art," no mere representational or logical fiction can pretend to authority. Only fiction exploiting the discontinuities and incongruities of experience can.

Yet even as Twain himself performs like Colonel Sellers, he retains the ambivalence implied by the story of Laura—the danger of unmasking the "real" self, whose roots go back to a lost childhood, a self without which, however, one becomes at best a Dilworthy (whose own self is hidden beneath the layers of Sunday School performances). The other alternative is to be Washington Hawkins, hardly to be taken seriously even in his newfound wisdom. By liberating himself from the Tennessee land at the end he achieves a happy ending that Laura does not, but in so doing he gives up those very hopes of ambition and authority to which Twain had devoted himself.

The final chapter of *The Gilded Age* is turned over to Warner's characters. Philip Sterling strikes it rich in a coal mine in Ilium. It is perhaps not irrelevant that in this jointly written novel the closest person to a hero—"for a real hero [one] would have to go elsewhere," but Philip at least was never "ashamed to stand up for the principles he learned from his mother" (217, 234)—achieves marriage, wealth, and status in connection with a coal mine. Twain not Warner married the daughter of a genteel coal magnate and established his social position from that point. Twain had unsuccessfully sought his fortune in mines, and had turned to writing and performing after his failure. At the end of *The Gilded Age* this "sterling" hero has won his lass, in fact has more than one in love with him, has made his fortune, and has subdued the threatening female. Ruth has sacrificed her career in medicine. No longer nursing Philip, she is now ill and dependent on him, "well nigh helpless."

The story of Philip and Ruth reorganizes the conditions of Twain's own life. Olivia's invalidism had long preceded her acquaintance with Twain's and her father through his fortune provided the young writer with his first business capital. The industrious Philip, however, helps a struggling Bolton back on his feet in the coal business, and Ruth is witty but submissive. By the end, fathers have been displaced, young men like Washington and Philip exert independent control over their lives, and threatening females like Laura and Ruth have been subdued or eliminated. Twain can "harass and excite the reader" at the very end with his power over the text. Political, religious, and literary authority have been satirized and undermined. Power depends on performance, but performance that incorporates the audience's own desires. The author's performance assimilates and controls all the other performances which it satirizes; it makes thematic use of the very romance it burlesques; it imitates the objects of its criticism; and it exploits the audience's fantasies even as it displays them.

On the other hand, dealing directly, even grotesquely, with contemporary political and economic situations seems to have discomforted Twain. Settings in the past and adolescent characters not only allowed fuller manipulation of audience in a day when nostalgia, escape, and sentimentality governed popular culture, but also allowed more flexible control over fable and theme. A built-in play between ironic condescension and sentimental identification with children, between romantic nostalgia for the past and criticism of backwardness, would in *Tom Sawyer, Huckleberry Finn,* and *The Prince and the Pauper* provide Twain with resources for popular successes and for leaving his "real meaning" undetermined by subsequent generations of readers.[12]

Notes

1. Indispensable to any work on *The Gilded Age* is Bryant Morey French, *Mark Twain and The Gilded Age* (Dallas: Southern Methodist UP, 1965). It includes full discussions of the literary parodies and of the political background to the satire.

2. On economic developments and related American political attitudes see Edward Chase Kirkland, *Industry Comes of Age* (New York: Holt, Rinehart and Winston, 1961).

3. Mark Twain and Charles Dudley Warner, *The Gilded Age: A Tale of To-Day*, ed. Bryant Morey French (Indianapolis: Bobbs-Merrill, 1972) 3. Further references are to this edition and are cited in the text.

4. The original manuscript less subtly continued: "The air was balmy, the cornstalks were bending under their rich freight, the gwano-beds were in bloom...." (Mark Twain Papers, Bancroft Library).

5. Another example: "These neighbors stood a few moments looking at the mail carrier reflectively while he talked; but fatigue soon began to show itself...."

6. Clemens often insisted that Sellers must be interpreted as a gentleman, not a villain or fool. A letter to Warner in June 1873 (Princeton University Library) insists on his courtliness and hospitableness, the absence from his character of vulgarity. Clemens was upset at times by stage presentations that came close to the distortion or caricature he feared. On the other hand, his protests at times seem a trifle disingenuous, for with a delicate verbal balance he has created in Sellers a gentleman-fool-mountebank very difficult to capture fully on stage. A set of character summaries, in Warner's handwriting (Mark Twin Memorial, Hartford), indicate Sellers was meant to be seen as a kind-hearted, over-imaginative visionary.

7. Wayne Mixon suggests that Sellers is meant to typify the New South with its commercial tone. See "Mark Twain, *The Gilded Age*, and the New South Movement," *Southern Humanities Review* 7 (1973): 403-09.

8. The manuscript has "Pomeroy" crossed out and "Dilworthy" inserted at several points. The standard discussions of the historical background are in French's book and in Albert R. Kitzhaber, "Mark Twain's Use of the Pomeroy Case in *The Gilded Age*," *Modern Language Quarterly* 15 (1954): 42-56. Other historical references such as "Charles Sumner" and "Credit Mobilier" were also altered in revision.

9. The child on whom Mrs. Oreille has been doting turns out to be a dog. An authorial footnote (255) draws attention not only to the silliness

of the dialogue, but to the thematic relevance of current literature as well as Washington social life to Twain's burlesque. Another dog mentioned is "Martin Farquhar Tupper," named after a popular sentimental writer.

10. William C. Spengemann criticizes Twain for being unable to handle the sexual implications of Laura's story. See Chapter 3 of *Mark Twain and the Backwoods Angel* (Kent, OH: Kent State UP, 1966). The manuscript of Chapter 34, however, is quite clear in its implications that Laura is exploiting her sex appeal for political advantage and that anti-male revenge is a dominant motive. Whether Clemens revised to align the text with genteel standards or to maintain sympathy for Laura is less clear (Mark Twain Papers, Bancroft Library). Trygve Thoreson attributes Laura's fall to a combination of selfishness and innocence. See "Mark Twain's Unsentimental Heroine," *South Carolina Review*, 14 (1982) 22-32. A significant recent comparison of Twain's and John William DeForest's treatment of sex and politics is Jean Demanuelli, "Politique et femmes fatales: Portraits d'intrigantes dans le roman du *Gilded Age*," in *Seminaires 1977*, ed. J. Beranger *et al.* (Talance: Univ. de Bordeaux, 1978) 151-76.

11. French's book sorts out the influences of three Laura's on her character: Laura Fair, notorious defendant in a San Francisco murder trial; Laura Wright, an attractive girl Clemens saw on a steamboat; and Annie Laura Hawkins, a childhood sweetheart.

12. The staff editing the Mark Twain Papers at the Bancroft Library, University of California—particularly Robert Hirst, Paul Machlis, and Patti Obert—were very helpful to me, and I wish to express my gratitude.

8

Huckleberry Finn:
The End Lies in the Beginning

The ending of *Huckleberry Finn* has generated more critical commentary over the last fifty years than any other part of the novel. Although defenses and justifications of the ending appear every year, the consensus still is that the ending does not work, that, as Leo Marx once wrote, "The flimsy devices of plot, the discordant farcical tone, and the disintegration of the major characters all betray the failure of the ending."[1] Much criticism of the ending, however, derives from attempts to impose upon it endings out of Romantic or Realistic traditions that are important to Twain as conventions to play off against not to fulfill. The conclusion of the story is actually a variation of its beginning, and is anticipated in the opening chapters. The book finally achieves a circular form that, in tension with the linear episodic dimension established on the trip down the river while Huck is "educated," provides much of its lasting resonance. The end of the book lies in its beginning.

Three basic weaknesses, different critics have asserted, detract from the conclusion's credibility. First, Jim just cannot be made free at the end by an arbitrary action. The whole ironic drift down the Mississippi River deeper into slave territory, not towards freedom, must end with Jim's being returned to slavery. His sale by those two fraudulent ruffians, the Duke and Dauphin, is a fit conclusion to Jim's horrifying story. To have had him freed, for no credible reason, by the villain of the book Miss Watson is to undermine his previous role as a dignified but estranged and potentially tragic character.[2] John Seelye would go even further and imply that since it is Jim who gives the book its tragic dimension he should fittingly die in the end.[3] Second, it is farcical to have Tom Sawyer, by the most unreasonable coincidence, reappear at the end, and run Jim through a series of melodramatic and tortuous shenanigans in a fraudulent attempt to help him escape. The book has been Huck's not Tom's. Tom is important at the beginning as a foil to Huck; he is a bookish, conventional ro-

93

mantic unlike the pragmatic, realistic Huck. The satiric episodes along the river, in fact, point up the absurdities in Tom's point of view. To allow Tom to control the action at the end is to undermine the whole center of the story. Thirdly, Huck's gradual education into moral awareness is denied. One difference between Tom and Huck has seemed to be Huck's potential to grow: Huck has imagination and is dynamic, Tom has only fancy and is static. All Huck learns from Jim, Mary Jane, and the many instances of man's inhumanity to man comes to nought if the implications of the book's ending are taken seriously.

James Cox argues that Twain's conclusion turns the ironies of the novel back on the reader, for we patronizingly impose on Huck a good northern conscience that neither Twain nor Huck gives us much reason to infer.[4] Tom's shabby adventure exposes the reader and the act of reading. If I may extend Cox's argument beyond his explicit statements, such an interpretation implies that a reader twists what he learns to accord with the conventions and codes by means of which he is able and willing to understand fictional experiences. Twain's entire fiction has been a probing, ironic study of conventions of behavior, fiction, and communication; and the final irony is directed against the action by the "addressee" necessary to complete the communication of the fictional text.[5] Although Cox is at times over-subtle in justifying particular passages in the conclusion, he is most sensitive to Twain's intelligent awareness of author-audience dynamics, an awareness Twain first developed on James Redpath's lecture circuit. In fact, one reason the complications of American Realism can be profoundly explored through combined study of James, Howells, and Twain is that James most seriously considered the role of the shaping artist in realistic fiction; Howells continually examined the relationship of context and social theme to realistic fiction (it was James, of course, who raised the serious post-Realism issue of psychological realism); and Twain had the keenest sense of the artist-dramatist-author-orator's relationship to his audience.

It is not easy, of course, to fit Twain into a conventional pigeonhole of American Realism, even though some consider him the original and typical American Realist. He does not set his stories in the contemporary world, as the other Realists all do. Almost all his fictions are set in the distant past (*The Prince and the Pauper*, *Joan of Arc*, *A Connecticut Yankee*, *The Mysterious Stranger*) or the past of his own youth. Those set in a "present" are deliberately non-realistic in the ways of the Colonel Sellers stories or the Hadleyburg fable or even the deliberate fictionalizing of the "non-fictional" *Roughing It*, *Innocents Abroad*, and *Life on the Mississippi*. Despite his close friendship with Howells, moreover, Twain had a sharper sense of the limitations of journalistic realism in fiction. He had always been a teller of "stretchers" who deliberately drew attention to the fictionality of his writings as his literary descendant William Faulkner would in the next century. In some ways, in fact, Howells is to Twain as Hemingway is to Faulkner. Howells and Hemingway were both in search of a new realism, though over fifty years the notion of what would achieve a new realism changed greatly. To Howells capturing as accurately as possible a representation of an observable world and making it meaningful was a crucial goal. To Hemingway presenting a scene without distortion so that a reader would experience the same feeling about it that the author had was a crucial goal. Neither Twain nor Faulkner worried much about the fictional world being nearly identical to an experiential world. Realism to them meant cutting through literary conventions and romantic notions of the self on the one hand, plus achieving emotional and imaginative credibility on the other. Howells and Hemingway would not have quarreled with those goals, of course, but they might have disagreed about the function and operation of fictional communication. They worked hard to hide the fictionality of their texts, as artificial as their styles may appear from a distance. Twain and Faulkner emphasized the fictionality of their works; and despite Twain's explicit criticism of the romance, both writers freely drew on conventions and techniques of both Romanticism and Realism. The categories themselves, in American literature, may be more usefully considered "not as sets of rules but as sets of expectations and possibilities," to adapt terms Stephen Orgel has recently used in describing the meaning of "tragedy" and "comedy" to Renaissance dramatists.[6]

Criticism of the ending of *Huckleberry Finn*, however, often depends on categories the novel does not fit or assumptions about people to which Twain does not subscribe. In most ways the ending is quite consistent with patterns established earlier. First, tragedy is not in order for Jim or the novel as a whole. Seelye's ending provides too easy a way out. It disposes of Jim gratuitously. Jim's death has no meaning in terms of an error in his character or a mistake he has made or the course of action on the river. On a social level it does not ring true either. Americans did not kill off blacks genocidally. Blacks were enslaved, "freed," and kept in a condition of oppression, manipulation, and dependency. The most important influence on Twain's final deployment of Jim was his return to the Mississippi Valley in 1882. His observation of the "New South" and postwar life in the settled towns of the area contributed not only to his completion of *Life on the Mississippi* and the satiric chapters in the middle of *Huckleberry Finn*, as has been frequently illustrated, but also provided his best first-hand view of the condition of Southern blacks after the War.

Jim has been freed by an action as arbitrary as that by which all the real slaves in the states of the Confederacy were freed. If Lincoln's Emancipation Proclamation was a calculated, utilitarian political act necessary for the salvation of the Union, in his eyes, then Miss Watson's deathbed manumission was a calculated, utilitarian personal act consistent with her character and apparently necessary in her eyes, at the moment of death, for her own religious salvation. But in neither case were the consequences "freedom" in any but the most technical sense. In most ways the ex-slaves were dependent on either the protection of the Freedmen's Bureau or, after 1877, the less sympathetic domination of white Southerners. Tom's abuse and manipulation of Jim is historically meaningful, for Jim's fate, Twain pessimistically implies, depends on the good will of people like Tom and the Phelpses—they are about as well as we can do. The final responses of Tom and the Phelpses capture in miniature a whole range of American responses to the freedman—from manipulation to buying off one's own guilt to ennobling the savage. Aunt Sally asks Tom:

> "Then what on earth did *you* want to set him free for, seeing he was already free?"
> "Well, that *is* a question, I must say; and *just* like women! Why, I wanted the *adventure* of it; . . ."[7]

Later Huck asks Tom "what was his idea, time of the evasion?—what it was he'd planned to do if the evasion worked all right and he managed to set a nigger free that was already free before?"

> And he said, what he had planned in his head, from the start, if we got Jim out all safe, was for us to run him down the river, on the raft, and have adventures plumb to the mouth of the river, and then tell him about his being free, and take him back up home on a steamboat, in style, and pay him for his lost time, and write word ahead and get out all the niggers around, and have them waltz him into town with a torchlight procession and a brass band, and then he would be a hero, and so would we....
> And we had him up to the sick-room; and had a high talk; and Tom give Jim forty dollars for being prisoner for us so patient, and doing it up so good, and Jim was pleased most to death..... (243-44)

As Tom's first act of the book is to play a trick on Jim, so is his final act. This one is more dangerous: as the two tricks are similar, so are they different. As the book is circular, it is also linear; this story of a boy's edcuation implies that the refuge and escapes of childhood do not last forever. Tom's early games with Jim and the Sunday School picnic are harmless. They are transformed in Pokeville, Bricksville, and elsewhere into adult frauds and disasters. At the Phelps Farm not Sunday School teachers but real bullets break up the caper; no one dies but clearly something has gone wrong.

It only appears that Tom is not a character in the center of the novel. He is actually the most important absent presence in the book. Huck's dramatically staged escape from Pap's cabin is done with reference to

Tom as the arbiter of all such performances: "I did wish Tom Sawyer was there, I knowed he would take an interest in this kind of business, and throw in the fancy touches. Nobody could spread himself like Tom Sawyer in such a thing as that" (29).[8] Both the Grangerfords and the Duke and Dauphin are alternate exposures of Tom's creed that to be a robber one must be respectable. The camp meeting in Pokeville is a variant of the Sunday School picnic, the printing-shop fraud a gloss on Tom's ransom notes and bookish models: the written word can be misused in a number of ways. The final adventure, at the Wilks home, is a fitting climax to the role-playing, lying, and dramatics of the journey. Huck, for the first time since his escape, plays an active role in a counter-performance of which Tom would surely be proud, and in a "moral" cause.

Huck's performances, however, are individual; he cannot, or does not control or manipulate others. As Cox argues, Huck is also the most passive of literary heroes. He initiates no actions, he has no ambitions, he acts on the basis of no ideals. He is not a quester, but an escaper. People act upon him—the Widow, Miss Watson, Pap, the Duke and Dauphin, Tom.[9] Yet Huck is also one of the two most important literary embodiments of American freedom, individualism, and non-conformity, the other being Thoreau. Whereas the narrator of Thoreau's books is ostensibly the author himself, however, the narrator of *Huckleberry Finn* is not Twain. Critics often reduce the distance between Twain and Huck as part of their reading strategy in order to simplify the satiric inversions of the opening chapters. Since one main purpose of these chapters is to invert the conventions of society, fiction, and language itself, the reader has every reason to make this identification. On the other hand, Twain continually provides signals that Huck has shortcomings marking him as an unsatisfactory norm of behavior. The novel is, more or less, the trying out of the proposition: Huckleberry Finn.

One of Huck's most humorous lines follows his first hearing of the story of Moses and the bullrushes:

> I was in a sweat to find out all about him; but by-and-by she let it out that Moses had been dead a considerable long time; so then I didn't care no more about him; because I don't take no stock in dead people. (4)

The story of Moses, however, as it continues, has a significant relationship to slavery and leading people out of slavery.[10] Huck's lack of interest in books about dead people is a token of his inability and unwillingness to learn from history and culture, to generalize from experience, and to act on the basis of general ideas. Huck is the perpetually Adamic figure renaming himself and redefining his values on the basis of each human experience. He is more free than anyone else from the rigidities and prejudices that are based on outworn conventions and abstractions. Though as a literary figure he is in part the conventional "good-bad boy," he can in the world of this novel respond to experience more naturally than anyone else. He must have, of course, the limitations of primitive, or Adamic, man—superstition and self-centeredness (11). Nor can Huck be free of the socially conditioned conscience which is the product of one's education in the broadest sense. Twain makes this point most clearly in relation to Huck's attitude towards slavery. Huck believes he is doing wrong in helping Jim escape—of course, as Cox says, we take his wrong as right—even though the personal attachment to Jim outweighs the mandate of his conscience. By the end of the book, despite his affection for Jim, he is no more convinced of the abstract wrong of slavery. Nor is he any more aware of the humanity of black people other than Jim. When Aunt Sally asks if anyone was hurt on the steamboat, Huck responds, "'No'm. Killed a nigger.'" Though Huck's entire story at this point is a fib, there is no reason to infer that the assumption behind the statement is not Huck's. If Twain was testing the validity of a new, empirical morality, he was also aware that empirical learning that cannot advance to the stage of generalizations will not help the individual overcome faulty generalizations that he cannot avoid assimilating in his youth.

The unstated horror in Huck's future is the possibility that thirty years down the road he may end up like Pap. Face-to-face they stand out for their differences: Pap is a mean-spirited drunkard full of vituperative bitterness and greediness. Yet Twain provides a series of parallels to emphasize similarities. The new judge's futile attempt to reform Pap is like Widow Douglas's civilizing of Huck. Pap's attack on Huck's book-learning is frighteningly reminiscent of Huck's own contempt earlier. Both are superstitious and enjoy the same sort of life—fishing, loafing, neglecting social relationships. Huck stays with Pap until he feels the cabin has become another prison; he runs away because it has become uncomfortable, like life at the Widow's or dress-up clothes. He lights out for the same reason he does so again at the very end—to continue as Huckleberry Finn. The jury is still out, Twain might have said, on whether Huck as adult can possibly remain Huck or must choose between being Pap or Tom Sawyer. The meaning of Huck as character depends on his relationship, associatively and contiguously, with other characters in the same text, as is true of all characters in all fictional texts. Huck has meaning by contrast with Tom and by contrast with Pap—but also by similarity to Pap. Tom has meaning by contrast with Huck, but also by similarity and contrast with so many manipulator-dramatists down the Mississippi River. One crucial question the book continually asks is what happens when the children grow up? The characters we meet throughout the book are in part transformations of the meaning of "Huck" and "Tom" in an adult world. By the end neither has achieved a promising transformation.

Huck's final shortcoming, and though it at first seems a strength it is not, is his inability to operate within a fictional world. As totally empirical, pragmatic realist, he allows no place for fiction—or dead people. When Huck scoffs at Tom's pretending that A-rabs and Spaniards are in the meadow, the reader nods along with Huck because by that time his voice is in control. A whole world of conventions, pretenses, and lies has been overthrown, and Tom's childish games can hardly survive such housecleaning. Tom's quixotic robbery, however, is such a game as every normal child then and now might well play. Huck's rather dense refusal to take part in the game, on the grounds that it is merely make-believe, indicates he has but one code within which he can operate, and that is based on a rather crude positivism. He applies the same pragmatic tests to prayer or game—consideration of consequences. Fishing line but no hook at least compromises the value of prayer. It is terrifying to apply the same logic to: "We played robber now and then about a month, and then I resigned. All the boys did. We hadn't robbed nobody, we hadn't killed any poeple, but only just pretended" (12). Huck's logic implies that had they robbed and killed real people, the game would have been worth playing. The Huck we know, to be sure, would have little stomach for such violence (of Pap we are not so sure); but Twain's double irony again punctures Huck's perspective on his world at the same time it satirizes Tom's. Huck can neither create nor work within a fictive world. Neither indirect nor deferred gratifications are available to him, only immediate experiential satisfactions. His limitations and strengths are intertwined, but he is vulnerable. Socialized beings, who must civilize him to eliminate his threat, can control him because of the same fiction-making and generalizing capacities he, either by chance or will, lacks.

Huck is finally no match for Tom in a social world; and Twain himself, as he admitted, is closer to Tom than to Huck. Huck is a projection of our fantasies; but Tom, because he can move between real and fictive worlds, is more flexible and can manipulate and control characters within his world. Tom controls the action at the end of the book because the Tom Sawyers always control the Huckleberry Finns so long as the Toms can convince the Hucks of the "realism" of the fictive games they are playing.

By means of three further developments Twain brings the ending of the novel full circle to its beginning. First, there are the two crucial pieces of information that have been hidden from Huck. Tom, for adventure, has not told him that Jim is free from slavery; Jim, whether out of sympathy or self-interest, has not told him that he is free from Pap. The irony of the quest for freedom that is really going deeper into slavery is redoubled by the irony that the journey to freedom is unnecessary. No one is actually "free," but escape was not going to achieve freedom. The outrageous coincidence by which Huck and Jim end up with Tom Sawyer's relatives is simply a fictional reminder that escaping the confinement of self and society cannot be a factor of spatial progress. As in *Roughing It*, the lesson is that Eden is closed, man must return to civilization. The social implications of Jim's condition and the existential implications of Huck's cannot be divorced from slavery and from Pap. What lies further down the road for each will in part be a factor of that which they thought they were escaping. What is more, there will be other crucial bits of information hidden from them along the way.

Second, Tom's control is challenged and broken by the intrusion of the "real world." He may have known Jim was really free and that therefore his games were make-believe; but since no one else at the Phelps farm knew it, they were all acting on the basis of different rules—Jim was an escaped slave. The lesson of Tom's error is twofold: fictions do not finally control reality, unless the fiction-maker first persuades those in his environment to accept the same codes and conventions. The evidence of the novel indicates that such persuasion is quite common, though the fictions may turn out to be both self- and other-destructive. By the end of the novel Twain has not resolved the dilemma of human manipulation. Man in society by definition plays roles, and some persons control the deployment of people and roles. The key to the moral and ethical nature of that control still seems to lie somewhere between the socially educated moral conscience and that romantic "x" quality that somehow helps the occasional individual break through dehumanizing conventions, unless that quality too is taught.[11]

Twain's increasing pessimism, in fact, seems in large part based on such epistemological uncertainty. Knowing moral "truth," by the time of *The Mysterious Stranger*, is no more uncertain than is knowing physical, empirical truth. What one senses, sees, is more a consequence of the forms and codes one has been conditioned to see by than of anything validatively "there." From another perspective, it is all a dream, a fiction. Even in *Huckleberry Finn*, the fulcrum between Twain's Horatian and Juvenalian satiric periods, this kind of perspectival relativism is asserted. Huck, Tom, and Jim have all had experiences, and each has learned according to his own character, formed it would seem by previous experiences more than innate universals. This was not a satisfactory conclusion for Twain, for his pessimism was the product of his American romanticism—as was true of many of his contemporaries and successors who dealt both explicitly and unconsciously with the confrontation between the Emersonian American self and an increasingly complicated social and economic network that Americans were developing—Howells, Adams, Dreiser, Norris, Frederic, and London, for example.

Twain's third complication at the end is Huck's reminder:

> Tom's most well, now, and got his bullet around his neck on a watch-guard for a watch, and is always seeing what time it is, and

so there ain't nothing more to write about, and I am rotten glad of it, because if I'd a knowed what a trouble it was to make a book I wouldn't a tackled it and ain't agoing to no more. (245)

Huck, the one person in the world least likely to write a book, has been writing the whole thing while resting at the Phelps farm. Beyond the rather superficial acceptance readers offer of such a device as a convention, it is clear that Twain is not simply using a convention.[12] Mark Twain the novelist, himself under a pseudonym, offers as narrator of his novel the anti-fictional Huck. Huck might lie or dramatize in order to survive, but he would not likely create any gratuitous fictions about dead or unreal people. The world of this book, moreover, is not only seen and judged through Huck's perceptions, but assumes its very reality through Huck's language.[13] So, paradoxically, Twain creates his greatest "stretcher" by means of a voice that denies fiction, that insists on limiting cognition to empirical perceptions and value to pragmatic consequences. Yet the very sequence of adventures Huck relates—"adventures" is Tom's usual word for fun not Huck's—is bizarre and improbable, hardly typical of everyday life, borrowed more from literary convention than real life. So a sequence of events that are both conventional yet unliterary are arranged and narrated by a boy who is anti-fictional in a language that is unliterary yet creates a world and a literature as it proceeds.

Twain had the genius to know that that is how it is done. Actually the book is very much about the language itself which creates Huck's world. Twain emphasizes this at the beginning in many ways: by his "Notice" threatening persons seeking motive, moral, and plot—that is meaning; by his "Explanatory" note on dialects; by Huck's radically vernacular voice; by the recurring comments on lying and truth; and by a series of inversions such as the following:

... but it was rough living in the house all the time, considering how dismal regular and decent the widow was in all her ways.... (3)

Tom Sawyer ... said he was going to start a band of robbers, and I might join if I would go back to the widow and be respectable. (3)

The widow she cried over me, and called me a poor lost lamb, and she called me a lot of other names, too, but she never meant no harm by it. (3)

... you had to wait for the widow to tuck down her head and grumble a little over the victuals, though there warn't really anything the matter with them. (3)

Not only is it important that Huck rejects the behavioral conventions, but also the very words themselves, and the behavior attached to them, are subverted in such passages. As the novel continues to be an exploration of the proposition "Huckleberry Finn," it is also an exploration of the language, codes, and signs by which the world that a Huckleberry enters takes on form and meaning. A substantial part of the book deals not only with language but also with names, signs (in more than one sense), clothes, gestures, letters, and other communication systems, which are perhaps the subject of another article than this. Finally, it is noteworthy that Twain, in an entirely different vein, was interested in some of the same questions about signs, communication, and meaning that began to perplex the pragmatic philosopher C. S. Peirce at the same time. Surely more is to follow on the interweaving of empiricism, pragmatism, and Realism in American literary and intellectual life after the Civil War.

Notes

1. Marx's article, "Mr. Eliot, Mr. Trilling, and *Huckleberry Finn*," first appeared in *American Scholar* 23 (1953): 423-40. It is reprinted, with much of the other controversy on this issue, in Claude M. Simpson, ed., *Twentieth Century Interpretations of* The Adventures of Huckleberry Finn (Englewood Cliffs, NJ: Prentice-Hall, 1968). Two insightful justifications of the ending are in George C. Carrington, Jr., *The Dramatic Unity of* Huckleberry Finn (Columbus: Ohio State UP, 1976); and Alfred J. Levy, "The Dramatic Integrity of Huck Finn," *Ball State University Forum* 20 (1979): 28-37.

2. Essentially this is Marx's argument, but it is similar to that of other critics.

3. John Seelye, *The True Adventures of Huckleberry Finn* (Evanston: Northwestern UP, 1969).

4. James M. Cox, *Mark Twain: The Fate of Humor* (Princeton: Princeton UP, 1966).

5. The term is borrowed, of course, from Roman Jakobson's model, as developed in "Concluding Statement: Linguistics and Poetics," in *Style in Language*, ed. T. Sebeok (Cambridge: MIT Press, 1960) 350-73. I allude to the model because *Huckleberry Finn* is potentially such a fertile work for exploring convolutions in the relationships, in fiction, between addresser (and narrator), addressee, message, referent, contact, and code.

6. Stephen Orgel, "Shakespeare and the Kinds of Drama," *Critical Inquiry* 6 (1979): 123. On Twain's notion of Realism, see Sherwood Cummings, "Mark Twain's Theory of Realism: or The Science of Piloting," *Studies in American Humor* 2 (1976): 209-21. On Twain's exploration of the possibility of countering a terrifying world by creating through a personal language a new vision of identity or reality, see the dissertation by Charles J. Shively, Jr., "The Magic Circle: Language,

Perception, and Reality in the Writings of Mark Twain," Diss. Washington, 1975.

7. Mark Twain, *Adventures of Huckleberry Finn*, ed. Henry Nash Smith (Boston: Riverside Editions, 1958) 241-42. Subsequent references are to this edition. William M. Gibson briefly suggests the idea that Twain was concerned in this novel with the post-Reconstruction South. See *The Art of Mark Twain* (New York: Oxford UP, 1976) 113. Two insightful articles on this general topic are by Neil Schmitz. See "Twain, *Huckleberry Finn*, and the Reconstruction," *American Studies* 12, No. 1 (1971): 59-67; and "The Paradox of Liberation in *Huckleberry Finn*," *Texas Studies in Language and Literature* 13 (1971): 125-36. Harold Beaver describes the book as a version of the slave narrative in "Run, Nigger, Run: *Adventures of Huckleberry Finn* as a Fugitive Narrative," *Journal of American Studies* 8 (1974): 339-61.

8. On Tom Sawyer see Judith Fetterley, "Disenchantment: Tom Sawyer in *Huckleberry Finn*," *PMLA* 87 (1974): 69-74; and Edward J. Piacentino, "The Ubiquitous Tom Sawyer: Another View of the Conclusion of *Huckleberry Finn*," *Cimarron Review* 37 (1976): 34-43.

9. For a related argument, but one that goes in a different direction, see David F. Burg, "Another View of *Huckleberry Finn*," *Nineteenth Century Fiction* 29 (1974): 299-319. Burg sees this as "a revolutionary novel" anticipating literary modernism and "contemporary novels of humor."

10. See Kenneth Seib, "Moses and the Bulrushes: A Note on *Huckleberry Finn*," *Mark Twain Journal* 18, No. 4 (1977): 13-14. For comments on Twain's reservations about Huck, see Harold H. Kolb, Jr., "Mark Twain, Huck Finn, and Jacob Blivens: Gilt-Edged, Tree-Calf Morality in *The Adventures of Huckleberry Finn*," *Virginia Quarterly Review* 55 (1979): 653-69.

11. The most valuable study of Twain's reading in Lecky, the backgrounds to his obsession with the moral conscience, and his sense of the limitations of intuitive morality is still Walter Blair, *Mark Twain and Huck Finn* (Berkeley: U of California P, 1960).

12. See Walter Blair, "Was *Huckleberry Finn* Written?" *Mark Twain Journal* 19, No. 4 (1979): 1-3.

13. See Cox's chapter on the novel, where he discusses the creative force of Twain's use of the vernacular. For a brief item on the first chapter's anticipation of the ending, see Eugene McNamara, "*Adventures of Huckleberry Finn*: Chapter One as Microcosm," *Mark Twain Journal* 18, No. 4 (1977): 17-18.

9

Tom, Huck, and the Young Pilot: Twain's Quest for Authority

More ink is spent disputing the unity of *Huckleberry Finn* than almost any other problem in American literature. Defenders of the novel's unity, whether formalists seeking patterns of order or traditionalists needing to justify a canonized text, have found clues in the river, the single narrative voice, the journey, Huck's character, and Twain's relationship to his audience. Their antagonists dwell on tonal inconsistency, Twain's denial of the maturity that Huck has achieved, the condescending handling of Jim's fate, and the inappropriateness of the slaveholding Phelpses as a final norm of behavior. James Cox explained but understated the extent to which Americans rewrite the text and the main character to suit their own needs and fantasies.[1] Perhaps more than any other character and book, Huckleberry Finn is protean Americana—an indeterminate communication with potential for sentimentalizing rebellion, and debunking it, for resolving and thereby sentimentalizing problems of the American artist, for identifying the author as a dangerous equalitarian, or an unfortunate racist, and for countless other readings and their opposites.

On the other hand, its companion book, *Tom Sawyer*, inspires no such complicated and contradictory exegesis. That, critics say, is because it is a less rich novel, because its main character is more static and less profoundly drawn, because it lacks the dimension of Huck's first-person narration. All that, of course, may be a way of saying that lacking the problematic inconsistency of Huck and the more variable responses intrinsic to most first-person narrative, it has less interpretive indeterminacy than *Huckleberry Finn*. It allows critics less freedom to revise and redesign the text according to their own needs. There is little evidence that Clemens took the writing of *Tom Sawyer* any less seriously. In fact for some time he was unsure whether he would even complete *Huckleberry Finn*; and but for his return to the Mississippi River area in 1882 it might well have remained to this day an uncompleted story, like

"Huck Finn and Tom Sawyer Among the Indians" or "Tom Sawyer's Conspiracy" or a number of other manuscripts.

Tom Sawyer, in fact, is often called Twain's best organized fiction, his most formally perfect novel. His longer works seem to have structural problems, and along with the number of incomplete manuscripts indicate the trouble he had conceptualizing full-length books. He often seems best in parts, scenes, satiric chapters, not in long works. He disavowed, of course, any intention of being a novelist, or even liking novels. He was always strong as a travel writer, and the unities of his works often derive from literal or figurative journeys. Books such as *Roughing It* and *A Tramp Abroad*—even *Innocents Abroad* and *Following the Equator*—start out with an intrinsic geographical unity that can underlie or can be counterpointed against thematic unities. Even so, they are full of many digressions and embedded narratives that do not detract from but enrich a book's quality, so that modern criteria for textual unity are suspended to appreciate Twain's performance. Many of his manifest fictions, moreover, as distinct from latent fictions such as *Roughing It* which poses as autobiography, settle into travel books in order to develop beyond initial scenes. *The Prince and the Pauper*, *Huckleberry Finn*, and *A Connecticut Yankee* at least fall into this category. Opening chapters of each establish thematic conflicts, generally revolving around power and insider-outsider relationships; but then in the second half Twain puts a main character—with an associate—on the road, as if only with that kind of space can he maintain the authorial freedom to develop his performance. *Huckleberry Finn* and *A Connecticut Yankee*, at least, are then marked by controversial conclusions that raise unanswered questions about central issues. *The Gilded Age*, partly because of the disconcerting disunities between Warner's and Twain's narratives, imperfectly mixes the centrifugal thrust of speculative finance and western frontiers with the centripetal force of corrupt politics and imitative Eastern social pretensions. *Pudd'nhead Wilson* has a focused setting; but while trying to gain flexibility through narrative counterpoint, Twain finally had to break off "Those Extraordinary Twins" as a separate work.

Tom Sawyer, however, has a clear denouement. It ends with rescue of the pretty heroine by the newly mature hero, perhaps not having needed quite the reformation of the rake in Augusta Jane Evans' popular *St. Elmo* but nonetheless a rascal now accepting his place in society and duly contemplating marriage, to Huck's chagrin. It ends with death of the murderous villain, after liberation of the wrongly accused defendent. It has the consistency of a child's perspective on experience, or at least of an adult's notion of a child's perspective, if not a unifying vernacular narrator. It puts the pieces of its puzzle in order, and addresses themes with continuity despite an episodic narrative.

Tom Sawyer, however, was not supposed to end the way it does. The top of the original manuscript indicates Twain planned a Bildungsroman, or at least a story carrying Tom through early manhood, far-flung adventures, and a return years later to his childhood home, doubtless sadder and wiser.[2] He rather early dropped that plan, though the travels of Tom, Huck, Hank, Joan, and other protagonists over thirty years indicate some of what he had in mind. The problem of continuing Tom's story into adulthood perplexed Twain while writing the book and afterwards, and although he often returned to his young characters he had decided that it would not do to use the Tom he had developed in that way.[3] Whether his main concern was one of creativity—problems he would have adapting the character to manhood, or of reception—problems audiences would have that might then affect their opinion of *Tom Sawyer* itself, is unclear. Whatever the reason, Tom was to remain an adolescent. He was not to be a revision of Copperfield or Nickleby or Pirrip though, since Twain generally achieved his successes from writing deliberately against prevailing forms such as travel books or sentimental tales, it is unlikely he would have simply written within a Dickensian convention. It was not likely, moreover, he would have centered adult conflicts in this novel anyway, for the displacement of themes tied to power, money, and sexuality onto childhood conflicts allowed him a useful freedom in narrative development. Even in *The Gilded Age*, where that freedom comes from exaggeration and non-realistic elements, he is a bit awkward in handling the sexual/pecuniary implications of Laura's story. Through Tom's story he can handle sexual conflict as puppy love, financial ambition as a treasure hunt, and self-determination as childhood prankishness. Their implications are muted yet latently unsettling. *Tom Sawyer* is not, like Aldrich's *Story of a Bad Boy*, a comic brief for the author's youth, in which the scars of childhood lie manifestly on the surface of the text. Rather it is an index to the ways in which the inseparability of sex, money, and control obsessed Twain, as well as to the strategies he developed for appealing to and utilizing similar concerns in his readers without alienating their interest.

The original manuscript apparently did not end the way the first edition did. In one letter Howells referred to a final chapter as something he did not like.[4] Twain's reply suggested that he dropped the chapter and that it covered Huck's new life with the Widow Douglas:

> Something told me that the book was done when I got to that point—& so the strong temptation to put Huck's life at the widow's into detail instead of generalizing it in a paragraph, was resisted.

If so the deleted chapter suggests less thematic resolution in Twain's own mind than does the published ending, which provides comic romantic resolutions of the sexual and financial themes and of Tom's development into a kind of maturity. To append a chapter in which Huck, the polar symbol of freedom from the responsibilites of society, marriage, and economy, may be assimilated, is to reopen Twain's dialectic, or at least to reestablish a condition of tension—Huck's conflict with social restraint—and to question the resolution promised by the cave chapters. Or, alternatively, it is to restore Falstaff to the court, that is to tame Huck and, in a way that even the ending of *Huckleberry Finn* does not trivialize what goes before, to trivialize his earlier thematic import. Whatever Twain wrote in that final chapter, at some point he understood the conclusion of *Tom Sawyer* not as simple resolution but as dissonant counterpoint between the willingly civilized Tom and the barbaric yawp of leather-stockinged Huck, threatened by all that Tom's growing up implies.

With that in mind, my intention is to suspend concern with the unity of *Huckleberry Finn*, to disrupt the unity of *Tom Sawyer*, and to consider *Tom Sawyer*, the first sixteen chapters of *Huckleberry Finn*, and to some extent "Old Times on the Mississippi" as a single text written between 1872 and 1876, overlapping in fact *The Gilded Age* both temporally and thematically. Our concern with the unity of *Huckleberry Finn* is understandable yet curious given the seven-year gap between composition of the two halves of the book. The second half, in fact, makes a different kind of sense when paired with the second half of *Life on the Mississippi*, with which it forms a rich exploration of Mississippi River country around 1880, not 1840. The first half, however, Twain wrote not long after completing *Tom Sawyer* and, from all indications, as a cadenza recapitulating and varying patterns in that story. In effect, both "Old Times" and *Huckleberry Finn* are continuations of *Tom Sawyer*. One carries the adventurous youth to maturity through a trade that disciplines him, allows him both glory and authority, and actually helped destroy the wild frontier to which Huck's character is tied. The other carries the free spirit away from both male and female authority figures to that same river and more or less leaves him there with no authorial decision as to what it will mean to light out for the territory. But then the narrator of "Old Times," so dutifully having learned the art and science of piloting, finds his own security gone when the railroads and the Civil War decimate the steamboat business. Perhaps it is Huck, Tom, and the young pilot who thereupon light out for the Washoe Territory at the start of *Roughing It*, and come back a writer, able to convert, through performance, all sorts of experience into successes. Huck at least, a bit incongruously, has turned to writing; and whether or not that is the only way to to be Huck Finn in nineteenth-century America, it is certainly the only way most fantasizing twentieth-century romantics would want to be Huck.

Tom Sawyer was written sporadically over several years, actually between 1870 and 1875; but probably the fictional diary of Billy Rogers courting Amy Lawrence (age eight), the embryo of the Tom-and-Becky romance, dates from 1870. Critics connect "Boy's Manuscript," so labeled by Albert Bigelow Paine, in some way to Twain's courtship of Olivia Langdon as self-ironic satire or gently comic puppy love. It is hazardous to draw many inferences from such a fragment, for Twain's rhetorical intentions are hardly laid bare; but the intense competitiveness of the "courtship," the links between Billy's lovelorn despair and his status among local boys and his "property" for which he loses interest— all that is curious, partly because it all plays a major role in *Tom Sawyer* and partly because it makes manifest the relations between sex, power, and money dramatized in *The Gilded Age*.

If, indeed, *Tom Sawyer* were to end with something like Chapter One of *Huckleberry Finn*, it would have an ironic circularity, for the opening scene of *Huckleberry Finn* is an overlay of the opening chapter of *Tom Sawyer*, with a thematically serious conflict replacing a playful squabble. It would also have a two-pronged, more ambivalent, ending with a tension like that between Laura's death and Philip's fortune in *The Gilded Age*, and between comparably multiple conclusions in Twain's other novels. By using the Huck-Widow material at the start of a new text, Twain effectively began to rewrite or at least to counterpoint the structure of *Tom Sawyer*. Both novels depend on a dialectic between the meanings of "Tom" and "Huck"; and the significance of the two in each book varies, partly according to the presence of a figure like Jim in *Huckleberry Finn*. Given the impulse on Twain's part to develop Huck's tale immediately after the completion of *Tom Sawyer*, moreover, one has even a clearer sense of the dialectic in his mind, especially since the creative block he had after Chapter 16 was a signal to him—against the conventions of fiction, however—that he really was at an appropriate ending, Huck's flight, the only satisfactory conclusion to a text in which Tom is growing up to social norms. In one sense "Huck Finn and Tom Sawyer Among the Indians" was a similar attempt in 1884 to counterpoint *Huckleberry Finn*: let us see not what happens if Huck joins Tom in respectability, but what happens if Tom joins Huck in the territory. The reasons for that book's incompleteness are not known. Speculation has revolved around Twain's unwillingness to continue a situation implying rape of a white woman by an Indian. It may also be that Twain found himself resorting to silly romantic formulas in the absence of any clear sense of what to do with the boys outside of a more settled society. He had little thematic material to develop, short of rewriting *The Prairie* with the pathos of a teenaged Leatherstocking.

Huckleberry Finn Chapters 1-16, however, does rewrite *Tom Sawyer*. It is nothing new to argue that both books are not only astonishing performances but foreground performance thematically. Success in Tom's world is largely a matter of performance, of self-fashioning, or of controlling the game.[5] In commentary on *Huckleberry Finn*, of course, Tom's performances are generally set against Huck's situational pragmatism. Just as significantly, in *Huckleberry Finn* Twain turns the world of *Tom Sawyer* itself into a performance. As so many critics note, the entire world of *Huckleberry Finn* gains its essence, its very reality, through Huck's language. But through the blend of authorial control and Finn-ish vernacular, Twain is able to manipulate the sentimental convention of child hero, the satiric convention of the innocent rustic observer, and the conventional indulgence of the first-person fictional narrator, in order to assure control of audience and theme. As *Roughing It* displays the conversion of financial failure into success through writing and performance, as *The Gilded Age* less confidently explores the problems of success and performance, so *Huckleberry Finn* manifests a kind of authorial control through performance of (and in) the world of Tom Sawyer—by the least likely P. T. Barnum in the lot.

At the same time it consummates Tom's story, however, it also counterpoints it. Both books emphasize relationships of power and powerlessness; but whereas Tom's life is one of establishing control over others, Huck's is an attempt to free himself from controls. The distinction is clear from the two opening scenes. Tom engages in a coded and pre-dictable dialogue with Aunt Polly over his chores and his schooling. Huck is less interested in winning a contest, in fact is willing to try the dumb books and manners, but simply does not like them. One can imagine Tom returning at the next opportunity to hookey and escaping chores not only because he dislikes work but also because he enjoys outsmarting his guardian, teacher, and friends. Not so Huck! For all of his life's being all play, there is really for Huck no sense of play or games as something distinct from a workaday world. For Tom religion, one social institution assimilating him, is an annoyance (boring sermons for which one devel-ops alternative pleasures, silly Sunday School teachers, frustrating cate-chism) but also a social opportunity. The winner of a Bible—no matter what the content of the prize—reaps glory; and the Church nurtures girls who will be morally and socially acceptable wives. For Huck those op-portunities are meaningless; and once both prayer and the story of Moses fail the pragmatic test, he cannot be bothered with religion. Similarly school: like boys in other "school" fiction of the day—*Dukesborough Tales, The Hoosier Schoolmaster, Story of a Bad Boy*—Tom finds school a burden, or rather Twain finds it an easy butt of conventional satire. On the other hand, it is where Tom conveniently meets his girl friends; and such things as reading have a demonstrated pragmatic value for him. In a childhood world, books provide him—however inaccurately—his means for controlling the gang. In an adult world, one infers, Tom at least has the option to be another Judge Thatcher because of such skills and to sep-arate himself from the likes of Pap Finn, Muff Potter, and Injun Joe. Huck has no such interests, whether because of genetic or environmental influence Twain leaves unspecified.

As Tom learns the skills and conventions of self-fashioning, performance, authority, and success, Huck asks only to be his "self," the major problematic term of the novel, its begged and unanswered question. The ending of *Huckleberry Finn* explores, of course, not only the difference between being "Tom" and being "Huck" and the pull on Huck to be Tom, but also the significance or even possibility of being Huck in any kind of social world. *Tom Sawyer* is a simpler book partly because the story of learning to be Tom is more conventional, clearer in its ontological if not its political implications. Unlike Tom's flight from Aunt Polly, Huck's flight from the Widow and Pap is permanent, serious. He does not, moreover, get into fights with other boys the way Tom does. One might suspect he is tough enough to whip the other boys, but for Huck fights, like flights, would be matters of serious survival, not ritual combat like Tom's matches. In the opening chapters of *Tom Sawyer*, however, Twain sets Tom in a whole series of power-oriented conflicts, coded ceremonies that are at the same time thematically serious because they imply the rules of the larger, the real adult world in which the author himself lives. His game of fibs and deceits with Aunt Polly anticipates other scenes of work, religion, and school in which Tom learns his true role, whereas Huck after that opening scene with the Widow and Miss Watson, never returns, for example, to education except in ironic scenes with Pap or Jim, or to organized religion and the Bible. Tom, however, will learn his lessons well. Verbal resources are what he will use with other friends in order to manage their playtimes, and the same sort of kidnap or battle scene is presented in both books—in *Tom Sawyer* apparently to illustrate Tom's virtuosity, in *Huckleberry Finn* apparently to indicate Huck's pragmatic realism against Tom's bookish romanticism. In *Tom Sawyer*, moreover, it follows the notorious whitewash hoax, in which Tom first demonstrates his managerial adroitness, getting everyone else to do the work while he accrues the profits. By the end of the book, in fact, he will be six thousand dollars richer without having done anything Aunt Polly might call work.

Huck shares the treasure with Tom, but before leaving society he will surrender his portion to Judge Thatcher. He does so to keep it from Pap, but he also does so before lighting out for the primitive world of rivers and rafts. The fortune carries with it an obligation to be civilized, to be somewhat like Tom. It also is connected with things like marriage and family. His own "family," in fact, would claim a right to it, thus the mission to Judge Thatcher. In Tom's story the treasure is directly connected to his courtship of Becky, not merely in implicit long-range terms of class, security, and marriage, but also because it is buried—and discovered—in the same cave in which Tom proves his manhood by protecting Becky and, figuratively, slaying the villain.

This is the world from which Huck is excluded. As much as Tom enjoys devilment with Huck, he also can draw invidious social distinctions between the Sawyers and Finns. In certain situations he does not want Huck around, and there is never a question of Huck's coming on the picnic. Huck is also outside the school-church-home-centered world of courtship and social performance. He is baffled by Tom's interest in marriage. He is removed from the sexual thematics of the book, for they have a social not a biological significance. When John Seelye rewrote *The True Adventures of Huckleberry Finn*, he thought it necessary to insert some sexual interest in his teenaged hero's character, specifically in the Mary Jane Wilks sequence, for Twain's omission of it was incredible, a sign of the author's prudishness.[6] What Seelye forgot was that sexuality is a part of *Tom Sawyer*, and that its exclusion from *Huckleberry Finn* may be deliberate and consistent with the distinction drawn between Tom and Huck in the earlier novel.

The significance of Tom, in fact, and of his growth depend on a dialectic between "Becky" and "Huck," domesticity and the territory, civilization and barbarism (or innocence). Supplementing Becky's significance, of course, are such figures as Aunt Polly and Judge Thatcher—taming Tom's wildness or his pretense of it, just as the world of Injun Joe is one in which Tom gets involved only when he is with Huck. Huck is Tom's Falstaff, that world he must experience, know, and then be able to control in order to achieve not only maturity but authority. He is also in a sense Twain's own Falstaff, the fantasy of innocence for the wild humorist of the Pacific slopes, without which he as a writer would be another tepid novelist of the kind he contemned but without controlling which he would certainly not have Olivia Langdon and Nook Farm.

Unlike "Boy's Manuscript," *Tom Sawyer* does not burlesque the adolescent courtship. It makes humor of Tom's pretentious pitch for the Sunday School prize and of the various tactics he and Becky use to manipulate each other, but it does not depend on grossly exaggerated behavior. In fact, it illustrates all too credibly some of the crueler, as well as the kinder, aspects of junior-high-school romance. Tom and Becky become nearly sadistic in struggling for control; and Twain's imagery suggests that at some level the affair, despite its conventional aspects, meant more to him than puppy love.

The initial meeting between Tom and Becky occurs after Tom has proven his masculine authority by whipping the new boy, by manipulating a flock of fence painters, and by an "intrepid" and successful confrontation with Polly. Safely "beyond the reach of capture and punishment," he goes to the "military" company, the army, of which he is "General," and wins "a great victory, after a long and hard battle" (TS 52). Seeing the new little blonde on the way home, however, the "hero fell without firing a shot," and Twain commences a pattern of military language that describes the courtship and reinforces its fundamental power struggle.

The military imagery, however, is also displaced by a rhetoric of performance; and as in so many of Twain's works a social or economic conflict is translated into terms of language, art, writing, and performance. Both Tom and Becky try to show off for each other, or manipulate feelings by pretending affection for someone like Alfred Temple. The courtship also has its morbid aspect. Not only are the illnesses of Tom and Becky tied to the ups and downs of their courtship, but Tom spends more time than Emmeline Grangerford dwelling on death. In the book's comic scenes he fantasizes his own death as a way to punish Aunt Polly and Becky; and in the potentially tragic cave scene he faces the danger of death in order to save Becky and their "marriage." In the epilogue Twain says that if these were adult characters he would finish up with a marriage; and in their darkest moments in the cave, when "to sit down was to invite death and shorten its pursuit," they partake together of a cake they call "our wedding cake" (TS 194).

The courtship, within an adolescent frame, develops through such sexual rhetoric: the torment and struggle for control, melancholic fantasies of death, the engagement sealed by a kiss and shared chewing gum, and the anatomy-book embarrassment. Together they cast eyes upon the picture of a "naked man"—a scene more explicitly and fully developed in the original manuscript. When as a consequence Tom proves his "nobility" by taking Becky's punishment for tearing the book, the tactical wiles of their courtship are ended. Now her masculine protector in a quasi-adult world, Tom is able to save Becky in the cave and by also securing financial stability, figuratively, to consummate their relationship.

Huck is also a hero of sorts at the end, but a less spectacular one. He saves not a young damsel-mistress but a middle-aged widow, and that not directly but by relaying information to a helpful Welshman. Even so, his act threatens to civilize him, and only when kidnapped by his father is he freed from such constraint. Pap is the counterpart of Judge Thatcher, the male force pulling Huck away from or toward society. Lacking the social, sexual, and economic ambitions of Tom, however, he cannot profit from his heroism or from performance. Originally Muff Potter's role was to be played by Pap Finn, who along with Injun Joe would have represented the sinister forces in *Tom Sawyer*. It is less likely Twain changed the name because he was planning another book, on Huck, as that the complications of having Huck's father part of the graveyard-murder-trial-cave sequence were more troublesome than helpful. Muff is liberated, as in a sense Jim will be in *Huckleberry Finn*, but Tom, not Huck, is the central figure in his freedom. Nor is Muff particularly a signifying character, as Injun Joe is; and in those sequences where the distinction between Tom and Huck is crucial, Huck's father would be a confusing factor. Later at Widow

Douglas', where Pap can be part of a central contrast, everything is different.

Injun Joe, however, is the villain of the romance, one whose significance is linked to his race for, as Mr. Jones says, "white men don't take that sort of revenge. But an Injun! That's a different matter altogether" (TS 184). He is associated with graveyards and crime, one who makes real in Chapter 9 the sort of dangers Tom has manipulated playfully in Chapter 3. Tom's test to win Becky, in a sense, is to show he can convert his child-world skills of piracy and chivalry into real-world skills of money-making and wife-protecting. The key to both is Injun Joe. The turning point is the trial. Tom's last-minute decision to blurt out the truth and implicate Joe is his assumption of manhood and a social role. Conversely in *Huckleberry Finn*, Huck's last-moment decision to hide the truth saves Jim in Chapter 16 and defines a social role for the anti-social Huck. Like Jim, Injun Joe seems to represent for Twain not only the outcast race but certain "dark" aspects of human experience—generally positive with Jim, negative with Joe—set against the socially civilized. That is, Twain as much as Cooper draws on conventional racial symbolism of the nineteenth century—with Joe as Magua, Jim as Chingachgook. He never allows a direct threat of Joe upon Becky—the kind of scene suggested in "Huck Finn and Tom Sawyer Among the Indians"—but he does counterpoint Tom's threatening adventures with Joe against both the courtship struggles and the playful adventures revolving around Jackson's Island and games of piracy. All three story lines then fuse in the cave scene, whose consequence is not only "marriage" and wealth but taming or destruction of the dark threat.

It seems gratuitous to offer a conventional psychoanalytic reading of the cave sequence, the cave "no man 'knew' ... Most of the young men knew a portion of it" (TS 196).[7] On the other hand, the entire sequence in Chapter 31—the caressing of Tom and Becky, their connecting of love with death, the developing pattern of dependency and protection, the wedding cake, their raging hunger, and the final threat of Injun Joe—all at the very least reaffirm the dark mystery of discovery implicit in the book's love story and social myth. It seems uncertain whether Twain particularly intended any kind of social allegory revolving around Indians, uncivilized boys, and Western settlements. It seems clearer that by turning to adolescents Twain found another means for exploring and commenting on the kinds of social themes he was using in *The Gilded Age*—relationships between money, class, power, authority, and sex. To a certain extent *Tom Sawyer* also gave him a strategy for the rest of his fiction—not the Dickensian strategy of authorial control through a contemporary world plus exaggeration, grotesques, and direct satire as in *The Gilded Age*, but a strategy of childhood worlds or distant imagined pasts not bound to contemporary readers' anxieties but allowing the flexibility of romance with the authority of moral fable. When joined in a career full of travel books, that themselves fuse empirical authority and performative license, they gave Twain a broadly based literary appeal yet one free from the traditional constraints of both "novel" and "poetry."

Tom Sawyer, after all, has ridiculed a whole series of conventional verbal forms—Sunday School stories, aphorisms, sermons and prayers, quack medical journals, declamatory schoolroom compositions, and romantic fiction. On the other hand, it implies that one with both verbal skill and stage presence can establish some authority, and that a well-handled lie, particularly "a magnanimous lie," has as much moral authority as "George Washington's lauded Truth about the hatchet!" In Tom's glory— the near-glory at church (Chapter 4), the glory at school (Chapter 18), the glory at the end (Chapter 35)—are born both the first half of *Huckleberry Finn* and, less directly, the first half of *Life on the Mississippi*. Huck is a part of Tom that resists assimilation, that even by the end of *Tom Sawyer* has fled to the "old empty hogsheads down beyond the abandoned slaughterhouse," for whom Tom's life "don't work ... It's awful to be tied up so." But he is also an unsophisticated audience that Tom is so skillful at manipulating. By the end of *Tom Sawyer* Tom has persuaded Huck to return to a life of respectable robbery, just as at the end of *Huckleberry Finn* he will manipulate Huck into unnecessary games with Jim's freedom. The closest Twain comes to turning the tables, one might say, is at the very end of *Huckleberry Finn* when we are reminded that it is Huck after all who has written the book, who has created Tom Sawyer, that the squatter has indeed created the dandy.

The first half of *Huckleberry Finn*, however, does provide for the escape of Huck that the final ending of *Tom Sawyer* negates. It is as appropriate to *Tom Sawyer*, after Tom's "marriage," as Falstaff's ouster is to the end of *2 Henry IV*. Freedom from both Widow Douglas and Pap Finn, of course, is just that and leaves the youth on his own in the wilderness as isolated as little Sarty Snopes at the end of Faulkner's "Barn Burning." Or at least alone until he discovers Jim; and in one sense it is just before that point that *Tom Sawyer* ends and a new book begins. It is not exactly the *Huckleberry Finn* we know, for that is as much about the Duke and Dauphin as Huck and Jim, but it is a new book that Twain was not really able to conceptualize then—and in effect ever.

As Huck flees down the river, moreover, so does the young man of "Old Times on the Mississippi." As Huck finds a Jim, however, one with whom he can only be a fellow outsider from a society to which neither belongs, the youth of "Old Times" finds a Judge Thatcher—in the person of Horace Bixby. As *Tom Sawyer* dramatizes heroism in a world of fantasy, "Old Times" delineates a kind of real-world heroism, a real possibility of reaping honor, glory, sexual admiration, and success through an actual recognized vocation. "Old Times" begins with a young man awed by false performances. On board the steamboat he is impressed by the majesty and power of the mate's profanity and yearns to "talk like that." He admires the watchman who pretends to nobility but is really a backwoods humbug. Only with pain does he realize that the real success and honor of a man like Bixby depends on substance, mastery, knowledge, and hard work not simply showmanship. It is Bixby who in Twain's prose comes to represent "performance" in both senses of the term; and in fact his outward demeanor, despite an ability to swear with the best, is not that of the frontier braggart but rather the cool "sprezzatura" we might almost say, of the dandy—the "easy difference" of a man with confidence based on the knowledge that he is the best at what he does. Thus Bixby as model, as norm, and thus the rather explicit connections in the text between piloting and writing.

To master piloting is to master a system of signs that communicate "the shape of the river." Not the almost right shape—as Twain once said "not the almost right word"—but the exact shape, "the exact spot and the exact marks."[8] Moreover, they change, for "you mustn't get the shoal soundings and marks of one trip mixed up with the shoal soundings and marks of another, either, for they're not often twice alike" (LM 43-44). For the youth, learning the river, unfortunately, is reading "a book that told me nothing" until Bixby advances "to bear a lesson on water-reading." Then, the "face of the water ... became a wonderful book—a book that was a dead language to the uneducated passenger, but which told its mind to me without reserve" (LM 47).

To master the book of the river, of course, is to drive the romance from it, to deal with it "as a science" and finally perhaps "to show ... what a wonderful science it is" (LM 49). Similarly writing would be for Twain anti-romantic, a kind of repudiation of the very romances that he enjoyed as a child and that Tom Sawyer exploits in a world of play. It would become a serious business, not simply in the sense of dealing with serious themes but in the sense of engaging in the world of commerce and literary marketplaces. It involves not only mastery and control of the signs of the river, but economic power of the kind the pilots' union fought for and won. Like piloting, writing requires astonishing memory, judgment, and courage. *Life on the Mississippi* is not an allegory of writing, but Twain's attention is as often on his ultimate profession as on his memory of his first profession. The pilot is, he says, the only entirely independent man on earth. Twain's language is almost that used to describe Huck on the raft. Writers, by contrast, are "manacled servants," obedient to the needs of patrons, kings, clergymen, and editors, forced to "modify" what they write because of social restrictions. The pilot, however, has "boundless authority." Not only commanding deferential treatment from officers and passengers and the courtesy of equals from captains and princes, pilots can also separate themselves from convention by an "irreverent independence." Twain himself, in fact, came to appreciate the pilot's peculiar status of being able to put his wishes "in the form of commands. It 'gravels' me, to this day, to put my will in the weak shape of a request, instead of launching it in the crisp language of an order" (LM 72).

The kind of authority and independence Twain was seeking as a writer in the 1870s was best embodied for him in the figure of the pilot. The independence, of course, was also embodied in the adolescent fantasy of "Huck Finn." In *Roughing It* personal financial failure in the mines gives way in the second half to success through verbal performance. Similarly the demise of piloting gives way in *Life on the Mississippi* to a second half in which Twain is the successful writer manipulating audiences and materials. Or, one might say, even in *Huckleberry Finn* Chapters 1-16 Huck's very narration signifies for Twain a fundamental conversion of experience into authorial performance, of literary conventions into an independent and original authorial voice, and of Tom Sawyer's heroic masculine maturity into a strategy for the adult world. In this sense *Huckleberry Finn*, with "Old Times on the Mississippi," complements and completes the dialectic of *Tom Sawyer*. On the other hand, when Twain returned to *Huckleberry Finn* and "Old Times" in the 1880s and provided them with very different continuations and closures, they became in effect quite different texts.

Notes

1. James M. Cox, *Mark Twain: The Fate of Humor* (Princeton: Princeton UP, 1966) 167-84.

2. The best study of and collection of materials on the genesis of the novel are in *The Adventures of Tom Sawyer*, ed. John C. Gerber, *et al.* (Berkeley: U of California P, 1980). That is also the source of further references to the text of the novel. The classic study of the book's form is Walter Blair, "On the Structure of *Tom Sawyer*," *Modern Philology* 37 (1939): 75-88. Also see Hamlin Hill, "The Composition and the Structure of *Tom Sawyer*," *American Literature* 32 (1961): 379-92.

3. See the letter of 5 July 1875 to Howells, printed in *The Selected Letters of Mark Twain*, ed. C. Neider (New York: Harper & Row, 1982) 86-87.

4. *Mark Twain-Howells Letters*, ed. Henry Nash Smith and W. M. Gibson (Cambridge: Harvard UP, 1960) 1: 110-13. Also see Bernard De-Voto, *Mark Twain at Work* (Cambridge: Harvard UP, 1942) 11.

5. My term and a small part of my model for "self-fashioning" are borrowed from the work of Stephen Greenblatt—for example,

Renaissance Self-Fashioning: From More to Shakespeare (Chicago: U of Chicago P, 1980).

6. See John Seelye, *The True Adventures of Huckleberry Finn* (Evanston: Northwestern UP, 1970).

7. On the other hand, no one has really done so, surprisingly. In fact, scholars are only beginning to explore those questions related to American Realism that lie at the intersection of social-psychoanalytical concerns and semiotic-narratological concerns.

8. *Life on the Mississippi* (New York: Bantam Classic edition, 1981). References are to this edition.

10

Huck and Tom in School:
Conflicting Freedoms and Values

No book in American culture has been more troublesome for free-speech advocates than the *Adventures of Huckleberry Finn.* Disdained and banned from time to time over the years because of its unconventional social perspective, its sanction of misbehavior and bad grammar, and in the South for its progressive racial attitudes, it gradually established a place as one of the revered classics of American literature. More recently, however, it has been questioned, paradoxically, for its racial stereotypes and, like other classic American works, for its status in a predominantly white male canon. A review of issues surrounding the book's history and continuing to stir up controversy will help focus some fundamental questions about freedom of speech and about the relationship between freedoms and a society's evolving definition of itself.

In 1985 the Library of Congress published a pamphlet entitled *Born to Trouble: One Hundred Years of* Huckleberry Finn. Actually a lecture by biographer Justin Kaplan, it records not the boy's misdemeanors, as Mark Twain did, but the book's run-ins with authorities and establishments such as school boards. As might be expected, moreover, it exonerates and justifies the book against the retarded and misguided apostles of darkness who would ban or censor or expurgate the text in some way. As a consequence, however, it may gloss over and minimize some significant questions about classroom instruction in literature that is offensive to one or another group in our society.

It is ironic that this classic, once censored for condoning irreverence, for using a tasteless vernacular, and for being too sympathetic to blacks, is now a hundred years later cited for its racism. The irony results in part from the privileged status accorded classics in our culture, which protects them from certain kinds of attack. For years, of course, the book was criticized for its troublesome ending. Critics, including Ernest Hemingway, called the ending inept and inappropriate, "just cheating," while others

justified it with equally compelling arguments. Such issues were connected primarily to questions of literary form.

Not so the issues raised by the Concord (Mass.) Public Library in that
center of freedom associated with the American Revolution, with
Thoreau, and with Emerson. Trustees there in 1885 banished the book as
"trash and suitable only for the slums."

> It deals with a series of adventures of a very low grade of morality;
> it is couched in the language of a rough dialect, and all through its
> pages there is a systematic use of bad grammar and an employment
> of rough, coarse, inelegant expressions. It is also very irreverent....
> It deals with a series of experiences that are certainly not elevating.
> The whole book is of a class that is more profitable for the slums
> than it is for respectable people, and is trash of the veriest sort.[1]

Although Twain said he was pleased, for the publicity would "sell 25,000
copies for us sure," he was also troubled, for despite his irreverence he
longed for respectability as a family man and citizen of Hartford and its
Nook Farm suburb where he lived with his beloved Olivia. Early in his
career, however, he had decided to publish with the profitable but socially
marginal subscription houses—including his own by the time of *Huckleberry Finn*—rather than with a respectable firm such as Harper's.
Thereby he gained some freedom from genteel literary conventions.

Clearly the Concord Library was not about to compromise its own
genteel patrons, any more than the Boston District Attorney a few years
earlier would have disregarded the needs of his genteel constituents when
he arranged for *Leaves of Grass* to be banned. Thus the ironies of traditions: America perhaps necessarily tames and domesticates its dangerous
writers—Emerson, Thoreau, Melville, Whitman, Twain, Dreiser, even
Richard Wright—in order to make them part of a grand tradition extolling
freedom and individualism and other mainstream ideas. Tamed, of course,
they are also less threatening to and subversive of current institutions.
They become part of a cultural tradition that centers some kinds of
experience while excluding others, that consists of works, in a new frame,
not so upsetting to later readers as they were to original readers. Literature
is then "rich" but harmless.

It was not so for the Concord librarians, nor for the North Carolina
Free Will Baptists who got so worked up in 1985 over Clyde Edgerton's
Raney, nor for community fathers and feminists who for different reasons
drive pornography theatres from their neighborhoods, nor for those black
Americans trying to remove *Huckleberry Finn* from high school curricula.
All these groups discuss the effects of books on audiences, an issue for
years dismissed from literary criticism. Most scholars today recognize the
significance of differences in the impact of a novel on and the interpretation of a novel by various groups; and the history of *Huckleberry Finn*

certainly does illustrate the proposition that novels—like the United States Constitution or laws in general—are not static objects with defined meanings, that meaning is not something lodged in the words on the page but rather surrounds a dynamic process connecting author, text, and reader. Meanings change because readers change over time and space, because connotations of words may vary, and because even if the actual words of a text do not change (as they might with the discovery of an editing error or a manuscript variant), the status of a work may change greatly. There is a difference between reading an unknown book by a little known author and reading a "masterpiece" by a writer your teacher calls a great American literary figure. One might recall Doris Lessing's recent experiment of sending two novels under a pseudonym to her publisher only to have them rejected.

The status of *Huckleberry Finn* in the classroom, however, has also been threatened recently by attacks on what has come to be called the existing "canon" for cultural study and even on canonicity itself. Most who today would revise the curriculum in the humanities, of course, would not oppose the teaching of any of those works, but would withdraw the privileged status of certain established works in the process of both broadening our notion of what kinds of materials can be included and altering our notion of how they might be taught. As a corollary they might suggest that the definition of a canon can be a process of implicit censorship, silencing at times parts of cultures in the act of establishing the definition of that culture. Their adversaries, and of course canon-revisers and canon-defenders are both diverse groups, resist the expansion of core reading lists beyond proven classics, the use of criteria for selection not connected to supposedly "universal" norms, and methods of instruction more governed by rhetoric than by formalism and traditional history.

Lynne Cheney, for example, has recently called the teaching of humanities in America chaotic and lacking in both moral and aesthetic norms.[2] Designating post-canonical curricula and post-structuralist criticism as the agendas of faculty who would narrowly politicize education for selfish ends, she pretends to an apolitical dedication to universal norms. Her statements and reports, of course, are highly political and ideological, marred more by their lack of a self-critical dimension than by the intrinsic weakness of her arguments. Like William Bennett and Allan Bloom, she seeks a restoration of a pre-1970s curriculum, at least in the humanities. It is not clear that she would strip the sciences of molecular biology, microcomputers, and big bangs; but knowledge in the humanities would not be allowed to progress, rather would be caught at a certain moment in history—perhaps the Eisenhower years.

The notion has long prevailed that the arts do not progress in the way science does, that modern plays are no better than classical ones. Be that as may be, knowledge about the arts does progress in the manner of a social science. Of late questions have been raised about our secular canon of artworks, and the process of canonization, comparable to those raised by the Higher Criticism a century ago about the Biblical canon and its establishment. At the same time, political movements have raised questions about the process through which cultural texts have been selected for secondary and post-secondary education. Not only the Civil Rights and women's movements in America, but the emergence and assertiveness of third-world cultures have had their impact on humanities curricula. Some of the consequences of all this, uncertainty about what our students should read and how it should be taught, help justify Cheney's desire to restore order and priorities and a sense of the sacredness of great books. All this may be ironic in a century which has so completely commodified art and culture; and anyway it is a desire as profoundly felt by at least as many liberals as reactionaries attracted to Bloom and Cheney. Such restoration is, however, probably not possible, or if possible only in a much modified form incorporating the lessons of recent cultural study and the consequences of contemporary world history. The revised "Western Civ" courses at Stanford hardly justify laments that standards have yielded to barbarism, but if pedagogy is adjusted along with reading lists the new courses will represent one attempt to redefine a rigorous curriculum for a generation alert to non-western achievements and to the rhetorical and ideological dimensions of all cultural study.

The furor about canons has also in the 1980s overlapped a series of cases involving censorship of works such as *Huckleberry Finn*. At issue is that possibility of canonization of literary texts being a form of implicit censorship, or silencing, of groups of voices—not necessarily for explicit or evil reasons but rather as part of a complex process of cultural, economic, and academic self-definition. Some of those minority voices are now being rediscovered and incorporated into revised canons or non-canonical curricula. Current criticism and pedagogy also emphasizes culture-specific meanings as well as universal meanings, and as a consequence books may appear to be less divorced from actual situations of readers and students and may appear to have actual rather than only academic consequences.

Behavior to a great extent derives from imitated cultural forms, from values implicit in social rituals and important works. Even television shows define models of behavior. The introduction of black situation comedies, partly an attempt to capture new markets for advertising, was potentially a healthy development. For several years, however, they had no strong positive black male figures, no Cosby. The only strong black males a black child would normally see on television were athletes and policemen. On situation comedies the father-figure tended to be white, absent, or a clown. All this was not without significance. In a society where race has been a marking, a defining social criterion, young blacks can go only so far in adopting role models from white characters, and they may be especially sensitive to the characterization of blacks in fiction they are told to read. If literature matters in the classroom, it must matter in part through ways in which teenagers interact with it and grapple with it. If they are troubled by repeated use of the word "nigger" in a book such as *Huckleberry Finn*, the problem may not be solved by a background lecture. If they are troubled by Twain's portrayal of Jim, perhaps they should be encouraged to articulate and develop their response. In some classes *Huckleberry Finn* has created such difficulties that teachers may not even want to try to overcome them, but may find more learning can take place if another novel is used; if that is not the case, classroom engagement with such issues can actually be quite rewarding.

As Kaplan shows, the book's problems go back a long ways. An article in 1907 showed that every year the novel had been "banned somewhere in the United States," Denver, Omaha, Brooklyn, or someplace else. Harper's once printed an expurgated version fit for boys and girls, perhaps not unlike the current versions of *Romeo and Juliet* marketed for classroom use—except that it was certainly not sex that was removed, for there was none in *Huckleberry Finn* to remove. The irreverence and bad grammar, however, were corrected, doubtless by the same folks who once had Dizzy Dean removed from baseball broadcasts for the bad effect his grammar had on young listeners.

The most recent problem with *Huckleberry Finn* goes back to the inception of the Civil Rights movement. The earliest public complaint came in 1957, when the NAACP denounced the book as "racially offensive" and encouraged several school districts to remove it from their curricula. Then as now the issues were the recurring use of the word "nigger" and stereotypical elements in the characterization of Jim.

For a quarter century the problem was off the front page. At a time of cooperation between blacks and liberal teachers, moreover, conflict over such a work would have been counter-productive, especially since *Huckleberry Finn* also had a liberalizing influence. For some people the complaints would have been silly and easily resolved. "Nigger," after all, was for Americans of Huck's time, around 1840, the equivalent of "slave." Miss Watson's "slave" and Miss Watson's "nigger" meant the same thing. Twain was not using the term out of racism or disrespect. Even in Twain's time readers would have known that Southerners a generation earlier mostly used the term "nigger." The modern black, said many teachers, need only be informed of the historical change in the word's usage. Secondly, although Jim consists partly of elements drawn from the minstrel darky, he is a most sympathetic character and one of the most positive black characters in nineteenth-century literature by black or white authors. There were few earlier models of black characters available, and elements of novels, including characterizations, depend more on earlier writing than on real-life sources. In any case, the argument ran, students could be shown that Jim provides the book its most tragic and moving dimension and raises it above the level of *Tom Sawyer*. Twain, moreover, was one of the more enlightened Americans of his day on racial matters, and, as black actor Meshach Taylor has said, *Huckleberry Finn* is "one of the most powerful statements against racism."[3] Twain was, of course, a racist in that he did not escape common white assumptions about a basic superiority of his own race; but it might have been hard to find many white Americans of his day whose racial attitudes would be more acceptable today. Twain is simply more vulnerable than other authors, because he did address the issue of racial oppression and therefore did create situations with black characters. It is important to help students discriminate between a searching work such as *Huckleberry Finn* and vicious novels such as those by Thomas Dixon popular seventy-five years ago. This does not, nevertheless, solve the problem of teaching *Huckleberry Finn* to youth so offended that coldly analytical historical background cannot remove their doubts.

The purported racism of the book resurfaced as an issue in the early 1980s. In 1985 the American Library Association reported that "at least a dozen incidents of censorship involving 'Huckleberry Finn' have been reported within the past five years."[4] One of the most heated controversies came, ironically, in the Mark Twain Intermediate School in Fairfax County, Virginia, in 1982. John H. Wallace, an administrative assistant in the school, had been active in the 1957 NAACP case, and now found a receptive audience for a case he had been making in school districts for three decades. He called *Huckleberry Finn* "racist trash" without "redeeming literary grace" and, while not winning his fight, did persuade his principal to recommend removal of the book.[5] The superintendent then overturned the decision and opted for the "proper instructional setting" for use of the book. It is not clear whether without Wallace's energy there would have been much of a case.

The next highly publicized episode took place in 1984 in Waukegan, Illinois, where a black alderman, Robert Evans, led a fight to remove *Huckleberry Finn* and *To Kill a Mockingbird* from the curriculum. He did not succeed, but a year later the struggle was joined over a planned production of a dramatic version of Twain's novel at the Goodman Theatre in Chicago. In the vanguard were both Evans and John Wallace, recently moved from Fairfax to Chicago, where he was employed by the School Board.[6] Wallace said the book should be burned, "if ever there was a book" that should be burned. Pap Finn's racist diatribe, he argued, could not be read satirically by black children, who learn the hard way that many Americans actually share Pap Finn's beliefs: "I don't care about the satirical meanings. I'm concerned about the way it comes across to black children. It has caused a great deal of trauma for black children."[7] Wallace, perhaps resigned to the book's survival, has edited his own version that eliminates use of the word "nigger" and derogatory elements in the characterization of Jim. If critics have panned his edition, it is still hard to fault Wallace's dedication to alleviating the unequal discomfort experienced by black children forced to read the novel, often by insensitive instructors.

Wallace was certainly in sympathy with a group of black parents in State College, Pennsylvania, who in 1984 demanded the community re-examine the place of *Huckleberry Finn* in the high-school curriculum. At that very time, coincidentally, Penn State was planning a major conference on "Huckleberry Finn and 100 Years of American Humor." Several panels were finally allocated to the problem of teaching the book in high schools. Comments on both sides were predictable. In one of the more effective arguments, however, Bradford Chambers, a New York City administrator, suggested the novel not be used for a while in some high schools because of the need for teachers to develop sophistication in presenting the issues. He called for a moratorium until schools develop a race-awareness program to guide white teachers and students to an understanding of what a black person's response might be. Chambers had a better sense of the pragmatics than did the other panelists, who tended towards either a simplistic "ban the book" or a simplistic attack on the censors.[8]

The most intense advocate of censorship was Margot Allen, a local parent incensed by scholars' neglect of racial issues in the book. Black students, she said, should "not have to silently bear the cost of everyone else enjoying Twain."[9] What finally surfaced was that in 1981 her son, the only black in his ninth-grade class, had been made to read aloud the part of Jim in class by a condescending and insensitive teacher. His mother had filed with the State Human Relations Commission a complaint that was not taken up until 1984. By then she was regretting her decision not to sue in the courts, and was leading the opposition to continued use of Twain's book in the classroom.

The obsession of John Wallace with this novel and the difficult personal experience of Margot Allen and her son do not reduce the validity of their claims that *Huckleberry Finn* may pose problems for black high school students. The issue was actually well addressed in the 1960s by the black scholar Donald Gibson, who in *English Journal* effectively justified black complaints but still defended classroom use if the book "is taught in all its complexity of thought and feeling, and if critics and teachers avoid making the same kinds of compromises Mark Twain made."[10] Gibson was in a sense suggesting there be a dimension of "higher criticism" in the teaching of Twain's novel, locating it rhetorically and ideologically as well as formally and thematically. Since that time such approaches to the teaching of literature generally have become more common; but they have also put a strain on the priestly function of the literature teacher in America. In this century, and especially with the rise of the academic profession of literary study, the literary tradition in some ways took the place of the Biblical tradition in cultural education. Poets and critics from Matthew Arnold through Wallace Stevens spoke of man's fiction-making and poetic imagination as helping make up for the loss of faith and the loss of centrality of religion. On the other hand from New Criticism to Structuralism to Post-Structuralism literary scholars and critics have aspired more and more to a methodology with the rigor and respect of those used by natural scientists.

The functions of literature departments today can often be divided into those of the priest, handing down the great tradition, and those of the scientist, exploring and explaining a work's production, its way of communicating, and its reception. In a broader sense, of course, good teachers always combine the roles of priest and scientist. Unless education is a self-contradiction, students should receive the best, aesthetically and ethically, from their traditions. At the same time, they must learn perspectives from which to analyze and improve on those traditions. While learning enough reverence to foster appreciation of values, they should also develop enough of that irreverence that Mark Twain called "the creator and protector of all human liberty."

Today irreverence toward a classic is common, and a "great book" is more vulnerable than before. This makes the teacher's job no easier. She or he has even more need today to preserve some roles of the priest, to get students interested in and engaged in reading, and in reading some of the exciting strong works of our culture. *Huckleberry Finn* is surely one of those. In some classes it may work with no problem, although if so offensive to a group as to be pedagogically counterproductive, it is not indispensable. In a class teachers might focus not only on the book formally, thematically, and historically, but also on the act of reading, to explore how and why parts of a book upset certain readers at certain times. Women have raised similar questions about a number of works in a largely male canon. Students can be encouraged to engage a book on their own terms, not led to believe there is a secret meaning that the teacher knows how to discover but they do not, like the priest whose knowledge of the church fathers makes him keeper of so many interpretive mysteries. Teachers, of course, do know more about how to find such things, for they have been learning the codes and conventions for years. More attention, in fact, to how books mean than to what a teacher believes they mean might better equip students not only to read novels and poems but also to maneuver and survive in a world in which language and rhetoric are powerful tools for social manipulation.

Those outside the classroom should remember that while censorship and book-burning are deplorable, those who would censor are at least taking books seriously, something for which many of us might devoutly pray. The process of cultural selection by those in a position to define canons and curricula, moreover, if not the same as censorship, can be similar to a process of censorship, albeit unintended. Because it is a silent censorship, libertarians should at least be aware of the processes by which a society determines the cultural texts its youth will study, the kinds of voices included and excluded. Freedoms have significance only within the range of available choices. The right to vote loses importance when the available options have been determined undemocratically. Freedom of religion would lose importance without diversity of religions. Freedom of speech, always compromised by other public goods such as freedom from libel and riots, only has meaning in terms of the breadth of situations in which one can speak freely. Freedom to read books has meaning only in terms of the books of which one is made aware.

Notes

1. Justin Kaplan, *Born to Trouble: One Hundred Years of* Huckleberry Finn (Washington: Library of Congress, 1985) 5.

2. Lynne Cheney, "Report to the President, the Congress, and the American People," *Chronicle of Higher Education* 21 September 1988: 417-23. Also see, in the same issue, B. T. Watkins and T. J. DeLoughry, "Endowment Chief Faults Teaching of Humanities."

3. E. R. Shipp, "A Century Later, Huck's Still Stirring Up Trouble," *New York Times* 4 February 1958: A8.

4. Hilary DeVries, "At 100, 'Huck Finn' is still causing trouble," *Christian Science Monitor* 15 March 1985: 6.

5. Howard Fields, "The First Amendment," *Publishers Weekly* 23 April 1982: 18. An editorial in the *New York Times* justifying the super-intendent's decision led to an interesting exchange of letters by Allen Ballard (9 May 1982: 20E) and Morton Fried (18 May: A22). Ballard, a black Professor of Political Science at CUNY, recited a painful childhood experience and called for limitations on the use of Twain's novel. Fried, a Professor of Anthropology at Columbia, replied that the book provides a good opportunity to discuss racism with high school students and that to remove it would be "a strategy of defeat in the crucial war on racism."

6. Shipp A8.

7. Shipp A8.

8. Scott Ott, "'Huck Finn' Even Stirs Up the Experts," *Centre Daily Times* (State College, PA) 28 April 1984: A1, A7. A related article appeared 27 April 1984: B1. Further comments by Chambers appeared in his "Scholars and *Huck Finn*: A New Look," *Interracial Books for Children* 15, No. 4 (1984): 12-13.

9. Ott A7.

10. Donald Gibson, "Mark Twain's Jim in the Classroom," *English Journal* 57 (1968): 196-99, 202. The debate was rather widespread at the time of the book's hundredth anniversary. Among those attacking the novel were Frederick Woodard of the University of Iowa and Julius Lester of Harvard. For a summary of issues see the *Chronicle of Higher Education* 12 March 1985: 8. For other perspectives see David Herreshoff, "Teaching Mark Twain in the 1960s, 1970s, and 1980s," *Monthly Review* June 1984: 38-45; Leo Marx, "Huck at 100," *Nation* 31 August 1985: 150-52; and a special Fall 1984 issue of the *Mark Twain Journal* with black writers discussing the novel. Also of interest is James M. Cox, "A Hard Book to Take," in *One Hundred Years of Huckleberry Finn*, ed. R. Sattelmeyer and J. D. Crowley (Columbia: U of Missouri P, 1985) 386-403. A feature on Wallace is Rogers Worthington, "Huck Finn Still Suspect at Age 100," *Chicago Tribune* 19 May 1985: II, 3.

11

Mark Twain Plays the Fool:
A Tramp Abroad

While poets have always struggled with the problem of their own cultural authority, nineteenth-century writers had to cope with two particular challenges to the epistemological and social significance of their poems and fictions. With the professionalization of academic disciplines studying philosophy and society, literary meaning became more problematic. As literary audiences changed and literature became a commodity to be bought and sold in the marketplace, writers became separated from the audiences on whom they depended for their success. The writer in America, moreover, had no such traditional role as had been granted the man of letters in England. Mark Twain and William Dean Howells both developed successful, albeit very different, strategies for coping with that situation. Twain depended not on a Realist aesthetic but rather on the power of the literary performer himself, on the manipulation of tone, and at times on the blurring of meanings.

The writer in Twain's world asserts his authority through outrageous control of the verbal performance itself. He sets and shifts at will the ground rules on which literary communication depends. The pattern can be seen in such early works as *Roughing It* and *The Gilded Age*, in which Twain manipulates tone in ambiguous ways and emphasizes verbal performance thematically, but it also continues throughout his career. My concern here is with *A Tramp Abroad*, an early to mid-career work belonging to Twain's favorite genre, the travel book. It has some of Twain's most delightful writing, often in embedded legends and anecdotes, but it is rarely discussed by scholars. It comes at a critical point in Twain's career, when he is unable to finish *Huck Finn*, is popular on the lecture circuit, but has no clear ideas for book-length projects. Between *Tom Sawyer* and *A Connecticut Yankee* actually there were the two split books—*Huck Finn* and *Life on the Mississippi*, both compounded of parts written in the mid-seventies and parts generated by

Twain's trip west in 1882; there was the quasi-juvenile *The Prince and the Pauper*; and that was it, except for *A Tramp Abroad*.

Twain always had a problem with closure, and almost all of his books break in half in one way or another. The travel book, of course, had a built-in conclusion, the end of the journey; and it provided him freedom to maneuver without requiring the architectonics of the traditional novel. Thus, even in the novels, the journeys of *A Connecticut Yankee* or *The Prince and the Pauper* or *Huckleberry Finn*, on which the author can perform while worrying little about the implications of a denouement. *A Tramp Abroad* was actually a difficult project to complete.[1] Twain's first writing about Europe since *Innocents Abroad*, it is remarkably different from that book yet comments on it by implication. It is much less the travel book, includes little commentary on Europe, and consists in large part of embedded tales and anecdotes, the sort of thing at which Twain was at his best. The narrative strategy and the voice that Twain develops in the book, moreover, inform the method in the second half of *Huckleberry Finn* and in *A Connecticut Yankee*, where the tone in many passages as well as the implications of the endings are so problematic for readers.

Manuscripts for the book provide the greatest challenge to Twain's editors.[2] Its unused parts form a potential text as long as *A Tramp Abroad* itself. Much of the deleted material is what one might expect from a travel book. There is an unfavorable essay on French national character, and much material comparing Americans favorably to the French, who are described as crude, unnatural, dishonest, and impure. The deletions reduce the amount of direct social commentary and make narratives even more dominant. Also deleted are chapters on Germany—on Hamburg, Heidelberg, and Munich—that include strong descriptive passages as well as a narrative on the Schefflers, a fraternity of coopers who once saved their town and remain a privileged group in Munich. Like the chapters on France, these remain part of a book written but not published. Also dropped is the preface. Prefaces are often important to Twain's books, may disrupt conventional reading practice or establish a tone for what follows. This book, however, opens with a title that is a deliberate pun. The preface was a gloss on the pun, and like any explanation of a joke was tactically unwise if not boring.

In *A Tramp Abroad* Twain adopts a voice that is not exactly that of the American innocent, morally superior; but because the narrator can be the butt of the book's jokes, it is closer to that of the fool, a kind of Groucho Marxian fool who can be laughed at but still remain master of ceremonies. It is a less unified and more playful voice, one little beholden to "fact" and able to move with dexterity between farce and exposition.[3]

The first half of *A Tramp Abroad*, often humorous, consists largely of embedded legends and episodes, with some satire on cultural conventions but without much on national character. In the first chapter Twain announces his literary purpose, in fact, not as an account but as a "spectacle" that he will furnish mankind of a "journey through Europe on foot."[4] Second, he states that his personal goal on the journey was the study of "art" and "language," in a way the central themes of the book. Third, for the first of many times, he decides on this "pedestrian trip" not to walk but to take the train out of Hamburg. Throughout the entire walking trip he walks very little, except for one night when, lost and in the dark, he walks "47 miles" around a chair in his bedroom. Continually he goes by vehicle to his destinations. Fourth, in Frankfort—a section much abbreviated—he retells the story of Charlemagne and the Saxons, a tale that, like the portrait of Stonewall Jackson's last interview with Lee in *Life on the Mississippi* (Ch. 44), suggests the indeterminacy of all narrative meaning. It is an incident that is said to have occurred in sixteen different places, and it is described as either a victory or a defeat, gained or avoided. Finally, the chapter concludes with "The Knave of Bergen," a tale in which a lowly executioner dances while masked with the queen, then by virtue of his charisma and eloquence can save his neck by persuading the Emperor not to kill him but to knight him. By calling the man "Sir" not "scoundrel," the court can decriminalize the insult to the queen and the reader can receive his first lesson in art and language.

The first three chapters, like so many of Twain's openings, set the ground rules for the text. The second chapter, set in Heidelberg but with most of the Heidelberg material excised, is best known for setting up Jim Baker's Blue Jay Yarn, one of Twain's tall tales, in which the performer also defines himself somewhere between the raconteur controlling his audience (as the jay controlled his, except for one Nova Scotia owl) and the innocent fool, not quite understanding what it is all about.

Chapters on dueling take up a good bit of the first part of the book and balance the satiric and the serious until the burlesque "Great French Duel," in which only the narrator is hurt, by a falling participant, and he the only man hurt in a French duel in forty years. This chapter ironically undermines much of what has just preceded and leaves Twain as the fool in control. Next, after a satiric poke at opera, operagoers, and audiences for *Lear*, which has its own wise fool, Twain slides into an autobiographical reminiscence of a bad performance.[5] As a child he once on a boat failed, with a false cry of "Fire," to make the passengers panic. Feeling embarrassed and rather like a fool, he had to slink off alone to his quarters. Then, as if to illustrate how one solves that kind of problem, Twain counters with the King of Bavaria, who as sole audience and producer of his own shows can totally control the performance and the audience response, and can even order a real flood when the script calls for rain on stage. Opera and playgoers who do not listen to performances they supposedly adore might take a lesson from "The Cave of the Specter," where poor Gertrude is killed by her lover because, with wool in his ears, he cannot recognize the words of her song or the voice of his beloved. On the other hand, the very next story, antithetically, tells of Lorelei and the song that lures sailors to destruction. Should one listen or not? Does the listener control or become controlled? By the end of the book, in fact, the power of readers and audiences, like the power of performers, will have become an issue.

Chapter 11 is specifically on art and language, and includes one of Twain's silly drawings and a reference to his "great" picture of Heidelberg Castle. Also there in Heilbroning he learns the legend of the faithful wives, who save their husbands by changing the meaning of "property carried on their backs" to include their doomed husbands, whom they successfully carry out of the besieged town. Its meaning is reasserted in the dining room when the head waiter improves the quality of his French wine by merely slapping on a new, "German" label, a miracle doubtless comparable to the better known one of loaves and fishes.

In Chapter 17, following the "Ancient Legend of the Rhine," Twain tells the tale of "The Spectacular Ruin" or Sir Wissenschaft. After scores of knights die contesting a fiery dragon, this quixotic fool comes along with his fire-extinguisher and, in the name of science one might say, extinguishes the enemy. Offered any reward of his choice, Sir Wissenschaft asks only for the kingdom's monopoly on spectacles, a central pun that Twain wisely leaves unglossed. To control a country's spectacles would be to control what and how it sees, its perceptions.[6]

Much of the rest of *A Tramp Abroad* disrupts our normal patterns of perception, yet also self-reflexively questions the implications of controlling performances and visions. The anecdote of Nicodemus Dodge (Ch. 23), an apparently ingenuous backwoods apprentice who reverses practical jokes played on him like the dandy with the squatter, is conventional Twain fare. "The Man Who Put Up at Gadsby's" (Ch. 26) suggests both the power of the storyteller and the pathos of the Washington patronage-seeker. But the "Legend of Dilsberg Castle" (Ch. 19), the tragic story of Conrad, a superstitious knight who goes mad when his friends' joke leaves him convinced his betrothed is dead, implies the danger among fools of uncontrolled performances.

By the end of Volume I, however, Twain is also one of the fools, the dandy as well as the squatter. To Twain the perpetrator of practical jokes is also the butt of someone else's larger joke; the director of the performance may well be a mere bit player in some larger production. In Lucerne a sharp young American woman turns the tables on the impertinent narrator, who pretends to be an acquaintance of hers. Not only is she more quick-witted but she does indeed remember a time that Mr. Twain actually wronged her. Afterwards, he admits, "I had been well scorched by the young woman. I would rather be scalped." Not long thereafter Twain and Harris make total fools of themselves by getting out of bed by mistake in the *evening* to watch the sun *come up* over the mountain. As Harris finally realizes, when the sun goes down, the "sun isn't the spectacle—it's us," for scores of "well dressed men and women" are "gawking up at us" and now have quite "a ridiculous spectacle to set down in their memorandum books."

Just prior to the American woman's coup, Twain has presented a coarse, aggressive, impertinent American, "Charley Adams," a ridiculous fool at that time but all too similar in retrospect to Twain's own impertinent, foolish appearance with the young woman. Just prior to the embarrassing sunset, moreover, he has treated with cruel contempt an American numbskull, who in retrospect appears hardly more foolish than the sunrise heroes. The significance of each character, like the significance of any literary sign, has changed with the addition of each new episode. No one's pretenses, moreover, are immune to ridicule—neither the ant, called a mere sham living on a false reputation, nor the author. A novel within the novel here is, in the same chapter, a skeleton for a "Black Forest Novel," a story which promises rewards to the man who can accumulate the largest pile of manure.

What then happens in Volume II revolves largely around tone, or the writer's tyranny over tone. Much of Volume II is farce, and blurs the boundaries between realism and farce, between the vicarious and the real. One of the book's final legends is that of Stammato, who in the fifteenth century was "allowed to view the riches of St. Mark" and embezzled millions of dollars in treasures. His demise resulted from his need to *tell* someone of his grand success. Having blown his cover, he was soon arrested, tried, and hanged. Twain scrupulously protected his cover.

In this second volume Twain is even more the master of ceremonies arranging his performers, albeit in the end being manipulated on the train by another strong willed woman. The volume opens with a restatement of the gap between reality and language, event and narration, travel and travel book. Four essential sights for any pedestrian tour of Europe cannot be neglected, so Twain simply sends Harris to view them and bring back "a written report ... for insertion in my book." Thus the "Official Report" following, although, since ostensibly not by Twain himself, also fair game for his satire of the pretensions and foreign terms in guidebooks. Satire and parody continue, though alternating with burlesque.

Perhaps the author's purpose is asserted most consistently through the vicarious pedestrianism. If he is not sending Harris as a substitute on some daring deed, he is hiring a vehicle in lieu of walking. He hires "a four-horse carriage ... exceedingly comfortable" over the Brunig Pass and sleeps through the good scenery at that. When close to Giesbach Falls, however, he cannot in good conscience go to see them for one must take a boat—and he has promised "to walk over Europe on foot, not skim over it in a boat." Soon thereafter with "a chance for a bloodthirsty adventure" climbing "the snowy mass of Great Altels," Twain sits down to read up on it, and from then on reading about the Alps will regularly substitute for climbing them, voyeurism for the thing itself. Climbing Mt. Zermett is a pleasure "confined strictly to people who can find pleasure in it. I have not jumped to this conclusion" (II: 101), he says. No, he "read several books and vicariously endured, for example, a terrifying near-fatal fall by one Mr. Whymper. Near the end, at Mont Blanc, he swears, "I would ascend Mont Blanc if it cost me my life." Harris was afraid, but I "said I would hold his hand all the way." Then Twain boldly puts his eye to the glass of the telescope and lets it climb above the crags and crevasses, resting on the way, until he actually sees the summit "bathed in the glory of the noon" (II: 201). One must be so careful for at times one has seen a "frightful tragedy" through "the Chamonix telescope." Not long before, he received a "document, signed and sealed by the authorities," that he "had made the ascent of the Riffelberg," another giant on his itinerary that he had managed to conquer only vicariously. But the written document, after all, "proves" something, as perhaps, one might say, a travel book in Twain's day might prove something.

In the second volume, of course, he does do some actual climbing but hardly any with a straight face. Or at least we read about little with a straight face. When Twain moves from vicarious pedestrianism to actual pedestrianism the scene turns into burlesque. Unlike the novelist and the conventional travel book writer, Twain flaunts the power of the romantic artist against both social convention and the aesthetic constraints of representationalism. Verbal success depends more on performance than on truth. One significant failure described in this section is the clergy—the irony of Harris being in truth Twain's friend Rev. Joe Twitchell notwithstanding. In Chapter 7 amid an attack on the anachronism of ringing church bells in a society with clocks, and of reading notices and hymn texts amid mass literacy, Twain contemns the average modern clergyman as "a very bad reader" and therefore a bad performer with, for example, no sense of "the exceeding value of pauses" or controlling an audience.

The point is most shockingly asserted in the same chapter when an eight-year-old girl running in play nearly tumbles to her death over a forty-foot "perpendicular wall" into a raging river. Harris understandably expresses relief and gratitude when she catches herself and, safe, returns to her play. Twain, however, argues that Harris is really manifesting his "contrary nature and inborn selfishness," and cares "not a straw for my feelings," for to Twain it all represents the "loss of such a literary plum." The tragedy would have been such good material for a book that the writer "should have gone into Baedeker and been immortal" (II: 98). Not always does Twain make his points so bluntly, but as with a play by Eugene O'Neill if you don't get the point the first time it will be repeated in different forms. And as the courier, we learn in Chapter 3, controls the real itinerary of the traveler, so the author controls, uses, and shapes the material of the travel book. The traveler responding to the girl as person and the writer appropriating her as material are different animals. Elsewhere Twain, for example, laments the loss of a person who "would have made an elegant paragraph" (II:80), but he also asserts his purpose through the continual exaggerations. When Twain actually prepares to climb the Riffelberg he enlists his party "of 198 persons, including the mules; or 205, including the cows." The staff list includes 15 barkeepers, 1 Latinist, 4 Pastry cooks ..., and the whole thing, as Twain and his party decide to "make the ascent in evening dress," has entered the realm of the absurd—quite specific satire on some actual contemporaries posing as hardy climbers but also a bit too ridiculous for the satire to remain in focus. Moreover, when Twain ties a half-mile rope to a guide and the guide subsequently deserts while tying it to "a very indignant old black ram," and the party is now lost, they are ready to murder the narrator until he is, luckily, kicked by the charging ram. The resulting humor saves both the situation and the hero. The scene has moved from satire to tall tale to reversal, all saved by humor.

Most of the rest of the book combines these three elements—satire, often on travel books, in which writer and reader mock a social or literary practice, tall tale in which writer asserts control over audience and text, and reversal in which writer becomes the fool, audience can feel superior, but writer in the process reasserts fuller control.[7] Several chapters revolve around silly "scientific" experiments with barometers and thermometers, the temperature of boiling water at various heights, the advantage to soup of the taste of boiled barometers, or boiled guides, and the pretentious use of pseudo-scientific notions and data, with the ostensible facts (II:155) being more outrageous than the obviously humorous exaggerations. Others revolve around tales of tragedy reappropriated for new purposes, or further vicarious absurdities—such as Harris testing a new means of descent—umbrellas used as parachutes, or Twain telescoping his way up Mont Blanc. Still others reassert the self-reflexive themes of the book. There is the story of little James, forbidden to play imaginary roles of steamboat captain or soldier and so playing God; or the story of Twain and the altar boy misunderstanding each other, the former sure he is being blamed for a niggling contribution, the latter vainly trying to return what is really too large a contribution. It all ends back in Italy, where, as in *Innocents Abroad*, Twain reflects on the Great Masters and galleries, confesses to some change in opinions yet still remains the brashly assertive innocent abroad unwilling to buy into established reputations, appropriating and controlling Europe as raw material for re-vision. Meanwhile this performance, that has combined satire, burlesque, tonal ambiguity, and manipulation of audience, along with a pseudo-foolish narrator, helps Twain develop the narrative methods he uses in the second half of *Huckleberry Finn* and then in *A Connecticut Yankee in King Arthur's Court.*

Notes

1. Justin Kaplan summarizes the problems Twain had with the trip and the book in *Mr. Clemens and Mark Twain* (New York: Simon & Schuster, 1966) 217-29.

2. I appreciate the help provided by Robert Hirst and by the staff at the Bancroft Library at the time I was using the Twain papers and manuscripts.

3. Louis J. Budd makes the point that *A Tramp Abroad* is less political than most travel books of the day, in *Mark Twain: Social Philosopher* (Bloomington: Indiana UP, 1962) 73-75.

4. Mark Twain, *A Tramp Abroad*, 2 vol. (New York: Harper & Brothers, 1907) 1:9. Further references are to this edition.

5. A letter to Howells, dated 30 January 1879, indicated Twain's hatred of travel, opera, and Old Masters was too great for him to write satire. Rather he could only "curse it and foam at the mouth." See *The Selected Letters of Mark Twain*, ed. Charles Neider (New York: Harper & Row, 1982) 109-10.

6. Pascal Covici, Jr., has discussed Twain's combination of parody with burlesque in "The Spectacular Ruin." See *Mark Twain's Humor* (Dallas: Southern Methodist UP, 1962) 118-22.

7. John Gerber, in discussing this book, is less sympathetic and argues that Twain burlesques his own material through a comic mask and thereby makes his narrative less credible and less interesting. He says, "Twain trivializes reality" with his clowning. See *Mark Twain* (Boston: Twayne, 1988) 78-81.

12

The Prince, the Pauper, the Writer, and Mark Twain

The Prince and the Pauper is a bothersome book for readers of Mark Twain. Not easily dismissed as a book for youth, because of its political themes, it lacks the seriousness and complexity to warrant extended analysis. It implies a moderately conservative politics at odds with a preferred image of Twain as anti-establishment gadfly. While it reaches a satisfactory resolution, and has a coherent structure, it goes beyond the length of a short story only by adding a loosely designed, almost picaresque journey.

In a recent article in *American Literature*, John Daniel Stahl, more coherently than anyone heretofore, has connected the central motifs of *The Prince and the Pauper* with Twain's primary fictional themes and recurrent personal obsessions.[1] Specifically Stahl explores the father-son relationships, the quest for lost fathers during which orphaned sons actually invent themselves, and the conflict between social circumstances and inner aspirations that defines the boundaries of such quests. In part he thereby frees the novel from its usual relegation to the status of work by the genteel hack-writer half of a divided author who reverted to "literary genius" when composing *Huckleberry Finn*.[2]

Stahl, however, amid a generally rigorous analytical framework, includes an apologetic subtext formalistically justifying *The Prince and the Pauper* as a good novel that is neither inconsistent homily nor mere children's book. As a consequence, he treats too narrowly several related issues that connect the novel to Twain's main concerns as a writer in 1880. These include Twain's ambivalence about his implied audience, his turn to a historical setting and continued use of a child protagonist, his concern at this time with the authority of writers as well as with political authority, and the multiple functions of Miles Hendon in the book. Not only a surrogate father for Tom Canty, Miles is also a displaced landholder, and finally an advisor-mediator, who may embody the interests and concerns of his author as fully as Tom and young Edward do.

In arguing the novel was intended for adults, Stahl emphasizes the subtitle, "A Tale for Young People of All Ages," without exploring the ambiguity of even that phrase. Whereas Twain, moreover, finally designated *Tom Sawyer* an adult book, whose perspective on childhood was that of an adult's memory, he dedicated *The Prince and the Pauper* to his daughters as a sign of a younger implied audience for that book and appreciated the enjoyment it brought local young people. On the other hand, it was admired and appreciated by many adults, and when Howells praised it he did so more for its picaresque and satiric dimensions, its allegory, than for its adolescent appeal.[3] To Twain's neighbors in Hartford, it had a respectability and moral seriousness that added a dimension to the author's reputation.[4] Twain had once considered anonymous publication, as he did with *Joan of Arc*, partly to protect *The Prince and the Pauper* from his reputation as a humorist.[5] Books were often published anonymously at that time; for example, Henry Adams' authorship of *Democracy* was one of Washington's worst kept secrets. *Democracy* was on the surface unlike Adams' other works, of course, though its values were consistent with them. Like *The Gilded Age*, it also had some potentially embarrassing characterizations based on real persons. Like *Democracy*, *The Prince and the Pauper* revolves around questions of power, morality, and legitimacy; but with no clear real-life antecedents it would have had less need for anonymity. Twain, to be sure, had conceived the tale as one about young Prince Albert Edward of his own time and wrote some twenty pages of a manuscript before changing his strategy.[6] Whether he thought twice about roughing up a living prince or found he needed the greater control over situation that a distancing historical strategy provided, he soon turned back to Tudor England.

It was his first experiment with historical fiction, a mode he then used frequently—in *A Connecticut Yankee*, *Joan of Arc*, and *The Mysterious Stranger*—and a natural device for one who liked the control that non-realistic strategies provided him over theme. Although he knew aspects of the mode from Renaissance drama, in his own century the historical *romance* had been primarily the genre of Sir Walter Scott and his followers. A form to be avoided, therefore, because of its connection with false Romanticism, it was based on a realism of researched detail, the politics of Tory values, and in Twain's mind Southern backwardness and phony chivalry. The form Twain developed was unlike Scott's fiction, for even when based on superficial mimesis his historical fables did not pretend verisimilitude. The form, however, did provide Twain a means to maintain ambivalence about social and political themes, as well as a good bit of creative flexibility.

In some ways, it is not necessary to revise conventional readings of the book. Edward does get an important education in real life. Becoming more street wise, he learns about poverty, injustice, and the need for a ruler to be open to many sources of information. Tom Canty does bring sound values to the palace and implies that royal ability need not be tied to royal birth. It is perhaps more interesting that Twain again resorts to child heroes, that he exploits the idealization of children common to his period, the period of Little Lord Fauntleroy and various Horatio Alger-type heroes.[7] By that device a writer assured readers' indulgence, sentimentally set youth against an establishment, and yet still could justify a conservative order. To most readers, Alger novels justified free-market capitalism as an open system of opportunity. *Fauntleroy* justified the English class system, if opened up to Anglo-American "natural aristocrats." *The Prince and the Pauper*, while admonishing the empowered to rule with mercy, fairness, and wisdom, and while challenging the philosophical basis of monarchy, did not finally challenge the pragmatics of monarchy from the perspective of democracy. The restoration of Edward is a positive good not a necessary evil. Order and justice are thereby restored.

A kind of Mugwump Republicanism governs. The party in power is probably best but needs to be more sensitive to increasing inequities and injustices. The anti-democratic notions of Twain continue to render ambivalent his democratic themes. As in American democratic thought back to Jefferson, and as in *A Connecticut Yankee*, mass man in *The Prince and the Pauper* is not to be trusted with power. The inspired youth Tom Canty, yes, but not the mobs and thieves and peasants and hermits one finds on travels through the country.

The story does contradict some of Twain's early tales. "The Story of the Bad Little Boy" and "The Story of the Good Little Boy" satirized not only Sunday School primers but also a set of moral tales suggesting that in our world virtue is rewarded, evil punished. In *The Prince and the Pauper*, however, criminals, conniving nobles, and rascally courtiers are all put in their place by the end. The virtuous characters are restored and rewarded, most likely one infers because of their virtue. Stripped of religious rhetoric, Twain's fable remains a bit like the stories he once parodied. In the 1860s he wrote as an outsider; by 1881, despite identifying with Tom Canty, he was much more the insider—at least in tales for edifying middle-class children. In effect Stahl does not really disprove Tom Towers' thesis that the book reflects a conservative streak in Twain's political philosophy.

By the middle of the book, at any rate, the moral points have been made, even if they are later re-emphasized. What become the centers of concern are the main characters' attempts *not to* be discovered or *to* be discovered. Tom Canty spends less time on justice in the kingdom than he does on maneuvering around the problem of being not to the manor born. On the one hand denying his royalty, on the other he learns as much as possible from his "sisters" and whipping boy in order to play his new role effectively. While Twain omits the differences in dialect and pronunciation that might uncover a Tom Canty, he does emphasize matters of style and gesture essential to maintaining disguise. Edward Tudor is less ambivalent than Tom about returning to his original status. The romance of poverty soon becomes as unattractive as the notion of returning to a frontier print shop or to a steamboat was for Twain himself.

As the author asserts, however, authority is largely a matter of appearance. The public can respond only to the conventional signs of authority. At the end, Edward's return to power depends on producing the great seal, the functional sign of royal authority, that which throughout the kingdom signifies an authorized act, such as the various restitutions made to deserving persons. On the road, however, he has little success persuading citizens that he is a king. The only system within which his declamations have meaning is madness: the tramps can condescendingly allow him to play prince, the mad hermit can seriously believe him and take revenge. In a sane world claims of royalty or nobility can have little authority. The world is full of impostors—Dukes and Dauphins—pretending royalty or nobility.

Twain himself was intrigued around 1880 by both con men and impostors, not only because of their prevalence in America and the frequency of nouveau riche sham but because of his own continuing concern with his ambivalent position as western humorist become famous writer, performer, and genteel New Englander. His embarrassing Whittier Birthday speech in 1877 would seem to have been intended as a mutually self-ironic joke among a group of fellow writers, its point being the necessary imposture for the writer in America. Each of his fellows—Emerson, Holmes, Longfellow—had in a sense developed a public mask for securing his place in American letters. Twain's was different, even more an imposture, but secured literary authority for him in a new generation. It is not so much that the old miner's visitors were not who they said they were, but that to be a writer was to split oneself in the way Twain suggested; and, as the miner's final question implies, the narrator is similarly vulnerable. The most significant aspect of the speech was not the apparent message, but the aggressive assertion by Twain that he was now part of that tradition. It was comparable to Howells' favorite story of Lowell's laying on of hands when Howells as a young man in 1860 had visited New England.[8]

From that point on, Twain's fiction revolved around impostors, changed roles, hidden identities, and fantasies of power. For every Duke or American Claimant or Mary Baker Eddy, there seems to be a Joan or Hank Morgan or Forty-Four who by supernatural powers gains astonishing authority. Twain's satire of phony authority complements an obsession with the control available to him as a writer and his own personal power. By his final decade he was combining rational attacks on Belgium's Leopold, Russia's Alexander, and America's Roosevelt with an irrational delight in being called "the King" in his own household.

The authority of Twain's new protagonists came to depend as much on writing and authorship as on other forms of action. Mary Baker Eddy's authority is intertwined with her own revised gospel, which transforms her into a messiah. Huck and Hank pen their own stories, and their *writing* of their stories is emphasized—Huck's at the end of his story, and also at the beginning where he specifically ties his text to a previous text, *The Adventures of Tom Sawyer*. Joan of Arc has her own Albert Paine, the Sieur Louis de Conte, but he is also the character representing Twain's interest in the writer as mediator for the man (or woman) of action, the person whose intercession is necessary for Joan's significance. He is also like Miles Hendon, declassé marginal figure but mediator for the powerful. Miles receives special status, comparable to that of the Fool, because of his role in the prince's self-definition. Miles enters the story at the moment of Henry's death, becoming like Jim to Huck the good father to shepherd Edward through danger, but also being restored to his rightful authority because of his special gifts as protector, interpreter, and mediator for the potentially powerful. If Twain projected himself through such ambitious manipulative performers as Colonel Sellers, Tom Sawyer, and Hank Morgan; if he projected himself through such innocents wandering through a corrupt world as Huck, Tom Canty, and Joan; he also projected himself through such marginal men as Jim, Miles, and Pudd'nhead Wilson, all of whom need protection of the truly powerful but all of whom also provide the moral norm for a text.

The Prince and the Pauper is a book about power, but also, if less clearly, a book about writing. It does not, like *The Gilded Age* or *A Tramp Abroad*, flaunt the writer's peculiar powers. Nor, as in *Huckleberry Finn*, does a novel being penned by an illiterate teenager muddy the clearer contrast between civilization and "the territory." It is more obviously concerned with control over the signs of authority, but writing has been rendered problematic in the preface. *The Prince and the Pauper* is introduced as a tale deriving from oral tradition, one whose truth depends not on distinguishing whether it came out of legend or history. That it "could have" happened governs its significance, the significance of the tale teller not the social scientist. It is a tale believed by the simple and unlearned (Twain's audience?), or by the wise (Twain's audience?)—all left very murky as in any Twain preface. Who knows who believed it? The only written documents in the prefatory matter, outside of the passage from Shakespeare, are printed and manuscript versions of the declaration of Edward's birth in 1537 and the royal seal—documents less significant for the reader, it would seem from the preface, than is the oral tradition.

Tom Canty, like Tom Sawyer, has gained what prestige he has from his knowledge of tales, from his reading. He has been taught by a good priest, whose narratives not whose sermons communicate his religion. The tales also provide Tom his own romance—to see a prince—that will carry him out of Offal Court and raise him to a higher class. Like Twain he can parlay a mastery of narrative, language, and performance into social advancement and a form of authority. If legitimate political authority is restored at the end, it has reshaped governance in accordance with the mercy of Tom, knowledge derived from observing poverty and injustice, and the humanity of Miles. It has provided a place, moreover, for both Tom and Miles and therefore everything they have signified in the book.[9]

Notes

1. John Daniel Stahl, "American Myth in European Disguise: Fathers and Sons in *The Prince and the Pauper*," *American Literature* 58 (May 1986): 203-16.

2. Stahl is responding in part to a position most recently and fully articulated by Tom H. Towers, "*The Prince and the Pauper*: Mark Twain's Once and Future King," *Studies in American Fiction* 6 (1978): 192-202.

3. W. D. Howells, *Selected Letters*, vol. 2 (Boston: Twayne, 1979) 271.

4. See the discussion in Kenneth R. Andrews, *Nook Farm: Mark Twain's Hartford Circle* (Cambridge: Harvard UP, 1950); and in Justin Kaplan, *Mr. Clemens and Mark Twain* (New York: Simon & Schuster, 1966).

5. The comment was made in a letter to Edwin Pond Parker of 24 December 1880 (Kaplan 238).

6. On the genesis of the book see the Introduction by Lin Salamo to *The Prince and the Pauper*, ed. Victor Fischer and Lin Salamo (Berkeley: U of California P, 1979). That edition is also the source of my references.

7. Twain sent Frances Burnett an inscribed copy of the book (Kaplan 239).

8. The episode is most fully recorded in *Literary Friends and Acquaintances* (Bloomington: Indiana UP, 1968) 35-38. Whatever actually happened and whatever its actual meaning to Howells in 1860—or to Lowell and Holmes, one might add—it later became for him a useful signifying event as he developed, in his autobiography, an account of American literary history with himself in the great tradition.

9. I am grateful for helpful comments made by Thomas A. Tenney on a draft of this article.

13

Life on the Mississippi:
Being Shifty in a New Country

In Chapter 44 of *Life on the Mississippi* Mark Twain briefly discusses an oil painting he observes in New Orleans.[1] Depicting Stonewall Jackson and Robert E. Lee on horseback, it is generally viewed as the "Last Interview between Lee and Jackson." Nonetheless, it might signify any of the following:

> First Interview between Lee and Jackson.
> Last Interview between Lee and Jackson.
> Jackson Introducing Himself to Lee.
> Jackson Accepting Lee's Invitation to Dinner.
> Jackson Declining Lee's Invitation to Dinner—with Thanks.
> Jackson Apologizing for a Heavy Defeat.
> Jackson Reporting a Great Victory.
> Jackson Asking Lee for a Match.

With neither title nor gloss it need not represent any one more than another. In Rome, Twain recalls, people "weep in front of the celebrated 'Beatrice Cenci the Day before Her Execution.' It shows what a label can do. If they did not know the picture, they would inspect it unmoved, and say, 'Young girl with hay fever; young girl with her head in a bag.'"

The indeterminacy of meaning in texts, a lesson embedded in this chapter, is also the central means by which Twain controls subject and audience. Unlike the indeterminacy of texts described by deconstructive criticism, it is a matter of deliberate method not just an intrinsic aspect of fictive discourse. Unlike Hawthorne, whose ambiguity is a matter of alternative readings of signs, Twain establishes control by shifting the terms of the discourse, even by implying contradictory codes.

Life on the Mississippi begins ostensibly, however, as a "standard work," a veracious travel book with historical backgrounds.[2] The hero of the book, the River itself, then turns out to be a deceptive and unreliable center. If over centuries it can radically alter its course, even overnight it can leave a man without a state. Similarly in *Huckleberry Finn* the river carrying a man to freedom really carries him deeper into slavery; the river liberating Huck from the confinement of "sivilization" carries him to the dregs of civilization. The narrator-protagonist of *Life on the Mississippi*, moreover, returns after twenty years not straightforwardly but in disguise, and continues to practice disguises. At other times he valorizes the successful actions of characters who deploy disguises (as in "The Professor's Yarn") and authenticates folk personae such as Uncle Mumford to comment to a society which repudiated the direct and often accurate criticisms of Frances Trollope and other visitors.

While using this kind of strategy, however, Twain also satirizes forms of sham, hypocrisy, and duplicity. The bogus sentiments and false values of a Sir Walter Confederacy, the veneer of the House Beautiful, the brutal treachery of John Murrell, the absurd extravagance of funeral customs—all are directly or implicitly condemned. Sham is repudiated; masks are justified. Similarly, in *Huckleberry Finn* one kind of lie is denounced, but Huck can only survive—and be sympathetic—by lying well. The dialectic, in effect, is shifted from Truth vs. Lie to Good Lie vs. Bad Lie. Moral lessons are denied by the author even as they are foregrounded in Huck's narrative. The author proclaims the use of multiple frontier dialects even as he authorizes a persona who would not know a pidgin from a creole.

Throughout his career, in addition to platform performances and marketing a public persona, there were at least three ways in which Clemens inscribed his own quest for authority and the dimension of power that accompanied it. In both *The Prince and the Pauper* and *A Connecticut Yankee* he directly dealt with themes of political power through fables of English kings. In both cases a powerless outsider through happenstance, shrewdness, and thespian skill insinuates himself into a position of power in such a way as to effect actual changes in governance. Whereas *The Prince and the Pauper* posits a merely temporary educative function for the role-playing outsider, *A Connecticut Yankee* implies more radical—although less sanguine—changes in the social order. Second, in tales set near his Mississippi River home, Twain fabricated a myth of childhood power—first in the form of the orphan boy who commands his own gang, rescues a heroine, and assimilates himself into the establishment; and subsequently in the form of the independent pariah who through his own vernacular controls a large fictive world that remains as indeterminate as "Lee and Jackson." Third, in the travel books, Twain confronted not only a long-established cultural, religious, and political order of the western world, but also a well-entrenched way of perceiving it. Through the voice of the "sophisticated innocent" he changed a basic conception of Europe and America while establishing himself as a new kind of authority, one who flaunted the fictiveness of his texts not merely their historical accuracy.

A trip west in 1882 provided Twain with the material and the momentum to complete both *Huckleberry Finn* and *Life on the Mississippi*. Each in its earlier form had been an initiation story, closely tied in Twain's mind to themes developed in *Tom Sawyer*. Similarly the second, or later, halves of both books share a number of concerns. Parallels and cross-references between the texts are frequent, and one chapter from a draft of *Huckleberry Finn* was even borrowed for use in *Life on the Mississippi*. Passages on feuds and false aristocracy, distortions of language and lying, scoundrels and disguises, the Missouri of Twain's youth and people named Finn, all echo the complementary text. Together the two texts also marked out a new phase in Twain's quest for literary authority. In one he empowered the voice of the innocent, the squatter, the tramp, which he had for years set up in opposition to established conventions, forms, and codes. By the paradoxes of literary conventions themselves, an ignorant ragamuffin governs not only a fictive world but audience response to it. In *Life on the Mississippi* Twain wrote a "standard work" that played fast and loose with empirical authority while centering a narrator who was not merely a traveler but Representative Man on the Mississippi River.

Both books were written amid a great deal of self-doubt, and Twain had recently struggled through an unproductive period. After piecing together *Tom Sawyer* in the mid-1870s he had been unable to finish *Huckleberry Finn*, to do much with a river book, or to develop his other projects. He labored with frustration over *A Tramp Abroad* and padded a slim tale to make *The Prince and the Pauper* publishable. From time to time he fancied himself more an entrepreneur than a writer, though fully aware his success and reputation depended on literature. Critics have argued that even if his wife Olivia and his friend Howells did not prudishly edit his fiction—and their suggestions were more often prudent than prudish—he was at best ambivalent toward the genteel Victorian lifestyle he had so zealously sought. Twain rarely had any public second thoughts about returning to the West or the river of the print shop and allowed romantic fantasies underlying his fiction to convey whatever nostalgia he bore in his soul. Thus the pattern of most artists who move into a higher social class by means of their art. They can indulge themselves without paying the price of atavism.

Everett Emerson has argued that *Huckleberry Finn* was to Twain a psychological release, an opportunity to vent pent-up frustration with his genteel lifestyle.[3] Of course, Huck's continual return to civilization, the implicit horror of an adult Huck turning out like Pap, and the underlying value of civilized progress beneath most of Twain's work including *Life on the Mississippi*, all render his indulgence in such a release largely a matter of play, if serious play. It becomes difficult to distinguish those parts of his innocent narrators attributable to his psychic defenses and those consequent upon his conscious literary strategies. If in *Huckleberry Finn* he can exploit innocence and the vernacular complexly and directly, in *Life on the Mississippi* he is more or less forced to retain the posture and voice of the sophisticated author.

Both books, however, do change directions around a crucial anti-authoritarian act. Huck is in flight from both male and female authority figures, but also is able to flee down the river because of a calculated and "bloody" escape from imprisonment by his father. Jim, of course, becomes a second and better father, and indeed Pap himself suffers a violent death about the time of Huck's escape. At the end Huck learns that both the male and female tyrants—Pap and Miss Watson—are dead. Only the more benign forces of civilization—Widow Douglas and the Phelpses—remain. The more profound fears of home are gone, and the Widow really does not restrict Huck's fundamental liberties any more than Olivia did her husband's.

The one story Twain added between "Old Times on the Mississippi" and those chapters narrating his return to the river in 1882 was the conflict between Mr. Brown and Henry Clemens, plus Henry's later death in a steamboat explosion. It is a curious addition, since Twain still does not provide information on the two years he spent as a licensed pilot prior to the War, and a general sense of the river's danger had emerged from earlier chapters. What it does allow is an intercession of Sam Clemens—who has been tutored by another good surrogate father, Bixby—to conquer heroically the false authority Brown and while rescuing the younger brother also to establish and rescue his self. The first half of the new *Life on the Mississippi* therefore not only narrates the coming of age of a persona in a soon outdated vocation but also dramatizes his usurpation of authority from one unworthy of it. The subsequent death of Henry, moreover, becomes a literary device signalling the end of a period, a phase of the hero's life.

Problems of authority, rebellion against authority, and unsatisfactory father-son relationships recur throughout Twain's prose. His heroes generally lack fathers, or have weak fathers, or like Tom Driscoll do not know their real father. In works like *Innocents Abroad* Twain undermines the foundations of authority or the Old Masters or thoughtless veneration of the powerful. Novels such as *A Connecticut Yankee* and *The Prince and the Pauper* challenge assumptions beneath a political order, but also suggest the basis for a new authority. *Huckleberry Finn* justifies rebellion against the tyranny of romantic convention and Sunday School lessons. When Twain, however, floundered in discovering a solution to his problem, his only solution was to reassert Huck's position as the *writer* of the text, to turn the squatter not into a dandy but into a writer. *Life on the*

Mississippi, somewhat like *A Tramp Abroad*, justifies the writer's rebellion against the tyranny of fact. As in *Roughing It*, moreover, the first half recounts a personal experience from youth—an attempt to get rich or find a career—and the second half deals with Twain's experiences as a writer, the vocation for one who has failed at other careers. The difference is that whereas in *Roughing It* the second half continues directly from the first, in *Life on the Mississippi* there is a twenty-one-year gap. Secondly, *Life on the Mississippi* does not re-address the problem of "becoming a writer" but recounts an experience of traveling specifically to take notes and write on America.

Unlike other books by Twain, this "standard work" has no confusing preface, only a quotation from *Harper's Magazine* emphasizing the vastness of the Mississippi Basin and symbolizing it as "the body of the nation."[4] The opening three chapters, however, which precede Twain's narrative of piloting on the river, provide a more extended overture to what follows. They give a sketchy historical chronicle on DeSoto, Marquette, and LaSalle, as well as the scene from *Huckleberry Finn* that is supposed to furnish a "glimpse of the departed raftsman and keelboatman which I desire to offer" (21). The tale of the Child of Calamity and a baby in a barrel is scarcely typical of anything, except of course "talk and manners aboard a keelboat" specifically as transmitted and interpreted through the vernacular of Huck; and language and interpretation become in the text even more important than fact and observation.

The historical chapters emphasize not only the vastness of the river but its mutability, and the necessity of contextual interpretation of facts. Facts are at best deceptive, from the beginning. They change over time. Cut-offs, for example, play "havoc with boundary lines" and can change one's state overnight. One cut-off "could have transferred a slave from Missouri" (such as Jim) "to Illinois and made a free man of him." Even facts specified by time have indefinite significance, for dates are relative to what surrounds them. Thus the connection of DeSoto's exploration with Luther, Michelangelo, Mary Queen of Scots, Charles V, and a legion of other Renaissance figures, as well as reminders of social and religious history. Thus also the explanation of the dearth of interest in the River between its discovery and its exploitation many years later, when it first became "useful." Similarly, the observations Twain makes along the river are included only as they become useful for his purposes. The actual opening of the land by LaSalle is described not merely as an "adventurous progress" but as a colossal robbery cloaked with "signs" of the Virgin, the cross, and the pipe of peace. Signs themselves, without interpretation, the author suggests, are as deceptive as facts. But, of course, Twain's method of interpretation is not that of "modern" novelists such as George Eliot and Henry James who, he once said, "bore" readers with their interminable interpretations, but rather that of narrative performance, of strategic lying to lure man out of falsifying frameworks. The French performances, we are told, "took place on the site of the future town of Napoleon, Arkansas, and there the first confiscation cross was raised on the banks of the great river" (9). Five times in one paragraph Twain reiterates the same phrase "the future Napoleon" not only to link by association settlement with martial conquest but also to set up a motif later echoed when the reader is told that the "future town" of Napoleon is now, in 1882, itself a past town that has disappeared into the Mississippi River (169).

"It is good to be shifty in a new country," says Simon Suggs. With rivers, towns, con artists, and businessmen coming and going, appearing and disappearing, the writer too must be a shifty entrepreneur. A fantasy of failing in one course of action followed by power through verbal performance governs many of Twain's books—*Roughing It*, *The Gilded Age*, *Life on the Mississippi* at least. Both *A Connecticut Yankee* and *Joan of Arc* end tragically, in a way, but posit authorship succeeding tragedy: Hank Morgan survives to write his own justification; Joan gets her very meaning through a verbal mediator. Tom Sawyer's maturity and conformity to society are answered by Huck Finn's controlling vernacular: authority is paradoxically achieved by adopting a voice that would deny authority.

In a sense Twain's original strategy in *Life on the Mississippi* is similar. By going aboard anonymously to learn as much as he can for purposes of writing, he yields up his authority temporarily. He adopts a disguise, not so he can learn "dull and ineffectual facts" but rather so he can be told the lies, the stretchers that passengers might not tell a famous writer. Good business for the writer is to learn as many good lies as he can. What Twain gets, however, are stretchers dredged up by Rob Styles just because he *does identify* the man as Mark Twain. Twain laments that although petty thieves may disguise themselves endlessly, when an honest man attempts an imposture he is exposed. Even in his own voice, however, Twain is "handier at lying" than Styles. Moreover, he is not through with his disguises: for the rest of the book he alternates his own with tales of other disguises and with other voices of authority such as Uncle Mumford and European travel books.

Late in the book, in Hannibal, Twain poses as a man named Smith. A native who might seem as able as Rob Styles to identify Twain does not and provides him therefore with candid sketches of village residents, their successes and failures. The episode is part of the narrator's return to and retrieval of his youth, which is significantly sandwiched between an assault on the South for its "Sir Walter disease" and some boosterish press releases for the Upper-River towns and their "go-ahead atmosphere" (270). Twain embeds his own youth between rejected feudalism and its sham sentimentality, its "house beautiful," and a progressive North, justifying thereby his own geographical dislocation. The oldtimer's line that Clemens was a "d—d fool," who would "have succeeded sooner" among the gullible fools in St. Louis merely underlines the significance to *Life on the Mississippi* of the embedded autobiography. It is also a reminder that Twain undermines the dichotomy between the Scott disease and progress even as he asserts it. If sham and falsehood are the villains of the piece, disguise and performance remain the heroes.

Notes

1. All references are to the Bantam Classic edition of *Life on the Mississippi*. At a conference on Dickens and Twain at the University of California-Santa Cruz in August 1984, J. Hillis Miller discussed this passage in a similar way.

2. The most thorough study of the composition of *Life on the Mississippi* is Horst H. Kruse, *Mark Twain and Life on the Mississippi* (Amherst: U of Massachusetts P, 1982).

3. Everett Emerson, *The Authentic Mark Twain: A Literary Biography of Samuel L. Clemens* (Philadelphia: U of Pennsylvania P, 1984).

4. On the functional importance of the appendix, see Richard Lettis, "The Appendix of *Life on the Mississippi*," *Mark Twain Journal* 21 (1982): 10-12.

14

The Troublesome Ending of
A Connecticut Yankee

The ending of *A Connecticut Yankee in King Arthur's Court* has been for many readers as troublesome as the ending of *Huckleberry Finn*. The Battle of the Sand Belt is an episode that if read seriously can undermine one's attitude toward Hank Morgan and therefore his narrative. Although some contemporary readers such as Howells apparently found it merely the conventional hyperbole of tall tale and fantasy, it does not really invite the whimsically ironic reading more appropriate to Hank Morgan's earlier permission for Morgan le Fay to execute a band of miserable musicians.[1] It seems dead serious, and is so tied up with the Interdict and civil war that are the climax to Hank's experiment in social engineering that a revised sense of its tone would necessitate a new interpretation of much else in the book. If Hank, hero of Arthur's "New Deal," can slaughter twenty-five thousand men at one time in order to perpetuate his system, he surely qualifies as one of the butchers of literature, and although Twain's destruction of Hank's new order may reflect Twain's ambivalence toward the technology beneath Hank's reforms, the massacre makes the hero and voice of the book even more problematic than the technology is and much more problematic than Huck Finn is when he helps Tom prolong Jim's captivity.[2] Actually it may not be possible to ascertain Twain's exact intentions with the Sand Belt; but it is possible, by connecting the social and artistic perspectives of *A Connecticut Yankee* to earlier and later works by Twain, to show that the ambiguous conclusion of this novel is symptomatic of Twain's general approach to fiction. Moreover, the actual ending of the novel is not the massacre. It consists of a postscript by Clarence, who preserves the manuscript, and a postscript by "M. T." who reads the manuscript. By means of a final scene of the stranger on his deathbed, Twain reminds his own reader that through the story its creator is alive at the time of creation and at the time of reception, that it can outlast many kingdoms and empires.

In one sense, of course, Hank's "New Deal" could not have succeeded, else how would Twain account for thirteen hundred years of very different history? The hero's death and a pessimistic conclusion, moreover, were two of Twain's first decisions, although in its early stages the manuscript had more of the levity of comic fantasy than the seriousness of social criticism.[3] Just as troublesome as the ending, moreover, is the role Twain assigns to the Church. The Established Church is blamed for every blessed wrong in England—poverty, cruelty, aristocracy, superstition, and general abuse of power. Yet for all practical purposes it never appears. There are a few priests, at times sympathetic, but no physical evidence of the Church, no character representing its power. The biggest mischief-maker is Merlin, hardly connected to the Church yet guilty of some of the same crimes. Otherwise there is this enormous power, capable of directing—through an Interdict—the story's conclusion, yet not involved in the book's drama or narrative. What makes the issue more perplexing is the relative impotence of the Church as a separate authority in Twain's own world. Not only was there no established church—and Twain praises America for that—but churches served the interests of the economically and socially powerful more often than the reverse was true. Outside of Twain's general predilection for satirizing churches and Sunday schools, and outside of a general point about the connection between religious institutions and power structures, it is not clear why Twain over and over hauls out the Church for his lashes. The book, to be sure, makes use of materials from different places, such as the fragment of a novel about Hawaii, responses to Matthew Arnold's criticism of America and George Kennan's portrayals of Tsarist Russia, and diverse political and social points Twain wanted to make; but while these explain certain inconsistencies in the text, they do not clarify the Church's role.

Thomas Fick has recently argued that Twain's concern with the Roman Catholic Church in particular was based on the connections between American Catholics and "practical" machine politics in large cities.[4] Hank's techno-politics provide a reformist alternative. Fick has to do some nimble footwork to avoid directly accusing Twain of xenophobia and anti-Catholicism, but his discussion is provocative; and while his thesis may not find general acceptance as an overview, he adds a dimension to our understanding of the book's political context. The American Catholic Church was not likely to become an established national church, corresponding to the feared Church in *A Connecticut Yankee*, but it may well have influenced Twain's composition in the same way that Kennan's articles on Russia did.

The power associated by Twain with the Church was held in America of the 1880s only by industrial and finance capitalism, a far less unitary institution than was an Established Church or monarchy. Twain's own

problems around 1888 revolved more around his money lost in the entrepreneurial and investment spheres than around any church, and as a
Yankee entrepreneur Twain would especially suffer when a newly
invented linotype machine put his Paige typesetter out of date almost
before it was built. Twain's other investments also fared poorly, and
while the forces of free-market capitalism hardly comprised a literal
Established Church, they did lead to some of the kinds of poverty
portrayed in *A Connecticut Yankee.* Nor was Twain, who always
identified himself more with the business world than with laboring
masses, of a single mind on capitalism. Over the years, he gradually
became more and more sympathetic to the plight of labor and to the
purpose of unions.[5] At one point he planned to include in *A Connecticut
Yankee* a more radical chapter, a critique of cruel and corrupt American
business practices (published finally as "Letter From the Recording
Angel" in *Harper's,* February 1946). Howard Baetzhold argues that it was
wise for Twain to drop the chapter, since "its attack on modern
capitalistic society would scarcely have comported with the Yankee's
several paeans to material and technological progress."[6] On the other
hand, with some revision in tone the chapter would give a fuller—if no
more lucid—picture of Twain's complex grouse against his world. All
this is not to say that Twain intended an allegory in which the Church
stood for capitalism, but rather that the eclectic social concerns running
through the book include some implied criticisms of the oppression of
labor and the poverty under American capitalism and also that Twain's
obsession with questions of power and authority is reflected in this book
in complex ways.

   Twain like Howells was understandably preoccupied with questions
about the authority of the writer and often demonstrated the writer's
power through various kinds of performance. But he was also
preoccupied with the themes of social and political power. *The Gilded
Age* is his only novel explicitly treating contemporary American politics.
Later in his career, however, he frequently dealt with royalty and
nobility—phony royalty in *Huckleberry Finn,* disguised royalty in *The
Prince and the Pauper,* royalty and its alternatives in *A Connecticut
Yankee,* lust for noble lineage in *The American Claimant.* After 1889
Twain wrote two kinds of books. Some revolved around detective
activity, the power of discovering secrets—at times with Tom and Huck
at the center but also in such forms as *Pudd'nhead Wilson* and the
unfinished "Which Was It?" Others centered directly around issues of
power. *Joan of Arc,* a generally neglected and not complex book, with
Twain's purest protagonist, cast the Church and autocracy more easily as
villains, although history did provide some constraints and the heroine
was assured martyrdom. Her execution at the end, terminating her
temporarily successful heroism, is parallel to Hank's long sleep after the

defeat of his reforms. Twain also spent many years on several versions of *The Mysterious Stranger*, including one with Huck and Tom, and was fascinated with the idea of Satan as hero and the corresponding diminishment of an authoritarian God. *Letters from the Earth* provides Twain's fullest challenge to a conventional theocentric view, but the Adam and Eve manuscripts are at least as significant to understanding this aspect of Twain's late prose. *The Mysterious Stranger* casts Satan as a proto-deconstructionist, undermining a metaphysics of presence. He delivers to mankind the message that men and their world are mere illusions without divine sponsorship. Finally, as curious an obsession as that with the Church in *A Connecticut Yankee* is Twain's fascination with Mary Baker Eddy and Christian Science. It was not just what he saw as a specious theology or the vulnerability of so many adherents to her pitch that fascinated Twain, but her phenomenal success and power, in a sense her performance. To him she was the most extraordinary woman ever, as tall as the Eiffel Tower or a Giant Sequoia. A strong businesswoman in a society of the dollar, she also created a new Bible, a new text, for her world and controlled its interpretation. By 1940, Twain whimsically predicted, she would control the United States and be the greatest religious force in the world, superseding the papacy. Like Twain's Satan, she is a more effective entrepreneur than Joan of Arc and Hank Morgan who, whatever their virtues, ambitions, and successes, could not control the institutions around them and thus were vulnerable in the end.

Power and authority are always, in Twain's world, factors of performance and control. In an early manuscript of *A Connecticut Yankee* Hank Morgan was to be storyteller to the King, and have access to the throne in that way.[7] Twain's revisions made Hank's authority stem less from verbal activity than from spectacle and popular entertainment, generally in competition with that mountebank of superstition, Merlin. Hank's successes come with such things as the eclipse, the explosion of Merlin's tower, the exploding pipe, the repair of the Holy Fountain—accompanied by assorted fireworks, and the use of a revolver. Hank's downfall ironically stems from his own overperformance with Dowley the blacksmith, when in an argument over the law he outwits Dowley, wins his case by trickery, but thereby terrifies and alienates his audience. They betray him, and before long Arthur and Hank, like Nigger Jim, have been sold into slavery. Hank has violated a cardinal rule of performance: know and consider your audience. Hank is later rescued by Lancelot in a scene no more convincing than Tom's "rescue" of Jim; but the final chapters seem as disconnected from the journey as the ending of *Huckleberry Finn* does from the trip down the Mississippi River.

Twain had altered his hero's name from Robert Smith to Hank Morgan. Thereby he provided his hero with the first name most commonly held by English Kings and in the surname connected him to Morgan le

Fay and thereby to her brother Arthur, establishing a royal lineage. Hank, who claims he will take no title from orders of the nobility but only that granted him by the people—"the Boss," sets out to overturn aristocracy but does so by establishing a parody of democratic capitalism in its place. It seems a parody because underneath it is not a free-market system but a centrally managed economy. Subjects are sent to "man-factories" and "teacher-factories" for re-education. The Civil Service Hank establishes is preferable to the system based on heredity and superstition. But, as in Edward Bellamy's *Looking Backward* of the same period, the reform system is imposed; the society is coerced into the reformer's frame. Hank has suggested that an earthly despot with "unlimited power" can be the best system of government even though in practice generally the worst.[8]

Hank's economic system is frequently mentioned albeit scarcely described. Hank has an entrepreneurial spirit (109) and, as The Boss, compares himself with one who has struck oil, better off than Joseph in the service of Pharaoh. At the beginning he finds he has "become a stockholder in a corporation" where nine hundred and ninety-four of every thousand members do the work while the other "six elected themselves a permanent board of directors and took all the dividends" (160). The rest of the book is dotted with discussions of currency, taxation, and stock markets. Knight-errantry is compared with a corner on the pork market (223). Pigs are bought at a price above their value on the commodity market (231). New coinage is compared with stock watering (300). Hank debates the relative merits of increased purchasing power and higher incomes, as well as the advantages of free trade and tariffs. Lancelot as President of the stock-board (the Knights of the Round Table reorganized) becomes a shrewd financier (446). But while there are these references to monetary matters, there is almost no further reference to underlying patterns of labor and production, not even any wordplay on the "Knights of Labor." Twain addresses poverty and injustice due to the old system of feudalism, the monarchy, and the church, at times, with implicit application to contemporary America; but what alternatives he would suggest, outside of generally more humane treatment of the have-nots, is fuzzy. Part of Twain's dilemma at the end of *A Connecticut Yankee*, of course, is that he simply does not know where to go. He has no model to dramatize as an alternative to what Hank found in Camelot.[9]

The structure of *A Connecticut Yankee* is actually like that of *Huckleberry Finn* (and, to some extent, *The Prince and the Pauper*). The first part presents a protagonist out of step with or alien to his environment, along with diverse humor, satire, and wordplay. The second part, following perhaps upon the author's running out of material to develop in the setting with which the book opens, consists of a journey involving the protagonist, true or ersatz royalty, and various rogues and incidents. The third part, following upon the journey running its course and someone being sold into slavery, is a somewhat clumsy attempt to resolve narrative and thematic problems. Criticism of the form of each book revolves around its ending and the troublesome implications for both the characterization of the protagonist and the author's social and ethical vision.

Justifications of both endings abound, and there is little reason simply to add another explication of the Battle of the Sand Belt, especially since Twain's ambivalence is as important as his craft. In *Huckleberry Finn* the ambivalence surfaces not only through the process of Huck's socialization but also, for example, in Twain's use of Colonel Sherburn, cold-blooded killer, as his mouthpiece to denigrate mass or mob man. In *A Connecticut Yankee* Twain waffles between democratic and antidemocratic sentiments, and also shows Hank to be often cruel and violent—hanging the poor musicians (198), suggesting the utility of a Reign of Terror and guillotine (not his choice, to be sure) for eliminating reactionaries (229), delighting in blowing up a pair of knights (318), and, of course, the final disaster.

It is easier always to describe what Twain does not like than what he likes. Moreover, the objects of his social criticism are diversely interpreted—England, France, feudalism, earlier ages in general, tyrannies in general, backwardness or its technological opposite when overdone. One might also see *A Connecticut Yankee* as a parable of America leading up to the Civil War, with the conflict between Yankee commerce and technology and a Southern-Sir-Walter-Scott-backward society culminating in general devastation. Slavery is occasionally a theme in the novel, and could be as convenient an allegorical reading of "The Church" as most of the others suggested. The Civil War, of course, was not totally out of Twain's mind in writing the book, but generally it comes to mind in reading such scenes as that of former knights selling sewing machines door to door as so many veterans of the war had done, at least when not selling, on subscription, books such as Twain's own novels.

I am not suggesting there is beneath *A Connecticut Yankee* a systematic allegory of America's "irrepressible conflict," but rather indicating that it is hard to pin down a single national or cultural referent for most of the social criticism in the book and that Twain did have conditions in nineteenth-century America on his mind as much as anything else. It is not, in fact, a social vision but the manuscript itself that is emphasized at the end of the text, a manuscript that with the help of Clarence survives. Not surprisingly several late works of Twain, whose early works so often deal with the authority of the writer, emphasize or are self-conscious about their own written texts. One can trace the pattern from *Huckleberry Finn*, in which, from the opening remarks by Huck about his creator and a previous novel to Huck's comments on finishing up the story, there is always beneath the surface the issue of the unlettered teenager crafting an artful verbal narrative. *A Connecticut Yankee* is ostensibly a document surviving since the days of Arthur. *Joan of Arc* is a verbal construction of The Sieur Louis de Conte, as he firmly reminds us at the end.[10] Mary Baker Eddy is fascinating in part because she displaces a sacred text with her own Bible. Twain's late texts about God are also about "writings"—*Letters from the Earth, The Diary of Adam and Eve.* In other stories it can be writing that disrupts and changes a community, as in "The Man That Corrupted Hadleyburg." More than any other writer, even Faulkner, Twain put writing at the center of his writing—as theme and as phenomenon. The authority of the writer and the power of the performer tie together his prose as much as any particular social vision does. The final point of *A Connecticut Yankee* is that Hank's political reform could not last; but his book survived for thirteen centuries. The aesthetic value behind the ending, of course, is the traditional one of art outlasting kingdoms and empires. The older Twain got, the more he was concerned about the survival of his works and his permanent position in American letters; and he seems finally to have found as much value in the authority deriving from permanence among serious readers as in any other role writing might have in his society. *A Connecticut Yankee* more or less picks up where *The Prince and the Pauper* leaves off. If an outside "advisor" combining characteristics of Miles Hendon and Tom Canty were actually to have a chance to help the monarch reform his kingdom, where would it lead? The author of *A Connecticut Yankee* was clearly less sanguine about such a political prospect in 1889 than he had been in 1880. Nor in any later work did he promise more optimism about social reform, although several of his works suggest the power of the written word to survive.

Notes

1. On contemporary responses see Henry Nash Smith, Introduction to *A Connecticut Yankee in King Arthur's Court*, ed. Bernard L. Stein (Berkeley: U of California P, 1979) 20-21. E. C. Stedman did persuade Twain to delete a description of a gruesome method of counting the bodies. This 1979 edition of the novel is the text on which my discussion is based.

2. The standard analysis that presents Twain as a progressive in support of technology and progress is Everett Carter, "The Meaning of *A Connecticut Yankee*," *American Literature* 50 (1978): 418-40. For different perspectives see Lorne Fienberg, "Twain's Connecticut Yankee: The Entrepreneur as Daimonic Hero," *Modern Fiction Studies* 28 (1982): 155-67; Richard S. Pressman, "A Connecticut Yankee in Merlin's Cave: The

Role of Contradiction in Mark Twain's Novel," *American Literary Realism 1870-1910* 16 (1983): 58-72; and Louis D. Rubin, *William Elliott Shoots a Bear* (Baton Rouge: Louisiana State UP, 1975) 52, 56.

3. On the genesis of the text, in addition to Smith's Introduction and the Textual Apparatus for the Iowa-California edition, consult Howard G. Baetzhold, *Mark Twain and John Bull* (Bloomington: Indiana UP, 1970) 102-61. Also see Baetzhold's earlier articles, "The Course of Composition of *A Connecticut Yankee*: A Reinterpretation," *American Literature* 33 (1961): 195-214; and "'The Autobiography of Sir Robert Smith of Camelot': Mark Twain's Original Plan for *A Connecticut Yankee*," *American Literature* 32 (1961): 456-61. A useful earlier article is John B. Hoben, "Mark Twain's *A Connecticut Yankee*: A Genetic Study," *American Literature* 18 (1946): 197-218. There is additional information in James Russell, "The Genesis, Sources, and Reputation of Mark Twain's *A Connecticut Yankee in King Arthur's Court*." Diss. (Chicago, 1966).

4. Thomas H. Fick, "Mark Twain's Machine Politics: Unmetaphoring in *A Connecticut Yankee in King Arthur's Court*," *American Literary Realism 1870-1910* 20 (1988): 30-42.

5. Baetzhold, "The Course of Composition" 5.

6. It is significant that of the first two books to analyze Twain's social ideas one, Philip Foner's *Mark Twain: Social Critic* (1958), described Twain as a latent radical, while the other, Louis Budd's *Mark Twain: Social Philosopher* (1962), discussed him as a moderate Republican.

7. Smith 7.

8. A provocative recent article on this topic is Jane Gardiner, "'A More Splendid Necromancy': Mark Twain's *A Connecticut Yankee* and the Electrical Revolution," *Studies in the Novel* 19 (1987): 448-58. She points out that science and technology in general would not during Twain's life have been considered like magic, quite the contrary, but that electricity—a kind of invisible power—was looked at very differently. Twain's ambivalence toward progress was connected, she argues, to the uncertain potential of electricity.

9. See Donald E. Winters, "The Utopianism of Survival: Bellamy's *Looking Backward* and Twain's *A Connecticut Yankee*," *American Studies* 21 (1980): 23-38.

10. See Susan K. Harris, "Narrative Structure in Mark Twain's *Joan of Arc*," *Journal of Narrative Technique* 12 (1982): 48-56. She argues that narrative is a central theme in the book.

Index